AN ESTATE PLANNER'S GUIDE TO

QUALIFIED RETIREMENT PLAN BENEFITS

FIFTH EDITION

LOUIS A. MEZZULLO

AN ESTATE PLANNER'S GUIDE TO

QUALIFIED RETIREMENT PLAN BENEFITS

FIFTH EDITION

SECTION OF REAL PROPERTY, PROBATE AND TRUST LAW
AMERICAN BAR ASSOCIATION

SECTION OF REAL PROPERTY | TRUST & ESTATE LAW

Defending Liberty
Pursuing Justice

Cover design by ABA Design

Printed in the United States of America.

20 19 18 17 16   5 4 3 2 1

ISBN: 978-1-63425-477-9

e-ISBN: 978-1-63425-478-6

Discounts are available for books ordered in bulk. Special consideration is given to state bars, CLE programs, and other bar-related organizations. Inquire at Book Publishing, ABA Publishing, American Bar Association, 321 N. Clark Street, Chicago, Illinois 60654-7598.

www.shopABA.org

This monograph is dedicated
to my wife, Judi,
whose patience, understanding,
and encouragement made it possible.

About the Author

Louis A. Mezzullo is a consulting partner in Withers Bergman LLP, practicing principally in California. His main areas of practice are taxation, estate and business planning, and employee benefit planning. He was an Adjunct Professor of Law at the University of Richmond Law School from 1978 to 2006, where he taught courses in those subjects; was on the faculty of the University of Miami School of Law Graduate Program in Estate Planning from 2004 until 2007; and was on the faculty of the University of San Diego School of Law in 2009. He is listed in *Who's Who in American Law, Who's Who in Emerging Leaders,* and *Who's Who in America* (Marquis Who's Who Publishers) and in *The Best Lawyers in America* (for tax, trusts and estates, and employee benefits; Woodward/White Publishers) and was listed as one of the top 50 lawyers in the 2012 edition of the *San Diego Super Lawyers* and in the "Top Attorneys in Business Services" in the *Corporate Counsel Edition of Super Lawyers*. He is listed in band 1, Wealth Management, Western Region, in Chambers USA 2015. He has written articles on the subjects of taxation, estate planning, and employee benefits for the *Journal of Taxation*, *University of Richmond Law Review*, *Virginia Bar Association Journal*, *Estate Planning*, *ACTEC Journal*, *Probate & Property*, *Taxation for Accountants*, *Taxation for Lawyers*, *Taxation of Employee Benefits*, *Journal of Passthrough Entities*, *Business Entities,* and *Trusts & Estates*. He has authored *An Estate Planner's Guide to Buy-Sell Agreements* (1st and 2nd editions), *An Estate Planner's Guide to Life Insurance* (1st and 2nd editions), *An Estate Planner's Guide to Qualified Retirement Plan Benefits* (1st, 2nd, 3rd, and 4th editions), *An Estate Planner's Guide to Family Business Entities* (1st, 2nd, and 3rd editions), and *Valuation Rules Under Chapter 14*, all published by the American Bar Association Section of Real Property, Trust and Estate Law. He has co-authored *Advising the Elderly Client*, published by Clark Boardman Callaghan; authored *Transfers of Interests in Family Entities Under Chapter 14: Sections 2701, 2703, and 2704*, 835 Tax Management Portfolio (3rd edition); *The Mobile Client: Tax, Community Property, etc.*, 803 Tax Management Portfolio; *Estate Planning for Owners of Closely Held Business Interests*, 809 Tax Management Portfolio (2nd edition); *Family Limited Partnerships and Limited Liability Companies,* 812 Tax Management Portfolio; *Estate and Gift Tax Issues for Employee Benefit Plans*, 378 Tax Management Portfolio (1st, 2nd, and 3rd editions); *Life Insurance,* 826-3rd Tax Management Portfolio (3rd edition); and *Valuation of Corporate* Stock, 831 Tax Management Portfolio (3rd edition), all published by the Bureau of National Affairs, Inc.; and was editor and co-author of *Limited Liability*

Companies in Virginia, published by the Virginia Law Foundation. He has spoken at numerous tax and estate planning conferences, including the Heckerling Institute on Estate Planning, the University of Southern California Institute on Federal Taxation, the Notre Dame Estate Planning Conference, the Mid-America Tax Conference, the Heart of America Tax Conference, the William and Mary Tax Conference, and the Virginia Federal Tax Conference.

Mezzullo received his J.D. from the University of Richmond Law School, and a B.A. and M.A. from the University of Maryland. He is a past Chair of the American College of Tax Counsel; a Fellow of the American Bar Foundation; a Fellow of the Virginia Law Foundation; a Past President of the American College of Trust and Estate Counsel, as well as former Chair of its Business Planning, Employee Benefits in Estate Planning, and Elder Law committees; a Charter Fellow of the American College of Employee Benefits Counsel; an Academician and a former Vice President of the International Academy of Trust and Estate Law; and a member of the Virginia State Bar; California State Bar, and American Bar Association, a former Vice-Chair of the ABA Section of Taxation, Chair of the Chapter 14 Subcommittee of the Estate and Gift Tax Committee of the ABA Section of Taxation, and a past Chair of the ABA Section of Real Property, Trust and Estate Law.

He is also a member of the Heckerling Institute on Estate Planning Advisory Committee, former Chair of the University of Richmond Estate Planning Advisory Council, former President of the Trust Administrator's Council of Richmond, and former co-director of the William and Mary Tax Conference. He is a former member of the Editorial Boards of the *ACTEC Journal,* the *Journal of Passthrough Entities,* and *Trusts & Estates* magazine, and former editor of *ACTEC Journal*.

Mezzullo is also a former member of the Board of Associates of the University of Richmond and former Chair of the Business Council of the Virginia Museum of Fine Arts and a former member of the Board of Directors of the Virginia Museum of Fine Arts Foundation. He is a former member of the Board of Directors of the San Diego YMCA and of the San Diego Opera. He is a former member of the Advisory Committee of the Virginia Opera, and a former member of the Board of Directors of the American Heart Association, Virginia Affiliate; the Richmond Symphony; the Richmond Ballet; and Willow Oaks Country Club. He was also President of the Southampton Citizens Association in 1972, and from 1985 to 1987.

Contents

PDF and Word versions of all the appendixes can be found at http://ambar.org/benefits5e.

Preface and Acknowledgments to the Fifth Edition

This fifth edition of *An Estate Planner's Guide to Qualified Retirement Plan Benefits* brings the first, second, third, and fourth editions current through October 2015.

Louis A. Mezzullo
November 2015

Preface and Acknowledgments to the Fourth Edition

This fourth edition of *An Estate Planner's Guide to Qualified Retirement Plan Benefits* brings the first, second, and third editions current through May 1, 2007. It reflects changes made by the Pension Protection Act of 2007 and the final regulations issued in April 2002, dealing with the required minimum distribution rules under Code § 401(a)(9), as well as a number of administrative pronouncements.

Louis A. Mezzullo
June 2007

Preface and Acknowledgments to the Third Edition

This third edition of *An Estate Planner's Guide to Qualified Retirement Plan Benefits* brings the first and second editions current through September 1, 2001. It reflects changes made by the Economic Growth and Tax Relief Reconciliation Act of 2001 and the proposed regulations issued in January 2001, dealing with the required minimum distribution rules under Code § 401(a)(9).

In preparing the third edition, Katherine E. Ramsey, an attorney with the firm of Mezzullo & Guare, PLC, reviewed the draft and made many valuable suggestions to improve accuracy and readability. My secretary, Pat Butler, was invaluable in completing the third edition. As I mentioned in the preface to the first edition, despite all this assistance, I remain the only guilty party for any errors or omissions (and would appreciate hearing about them from the reader).

Louis A. Mezzullo
October 2001

Preface and Acknowledgments to the Second Edition

This second edition of *An Estate Planner's Guide to Qualified Retirement Plan Benefits* brings the first edition current through October 21, 1997. It reflects changes made by the Unemployment Amendments of 1992, the Small Business Job Protection Act of 1996, and the Taxpayer Relief Act of 1997 (including a pending Tax Technical Corrections Act of 1997 which has been passed by the House Committee on Ways and Means) as well as case law and regulatory changes made since the first edition, including the Supreme Court's decision in *Boggs v. Boggs,* 117 S. Ct. 1754 (1997). In addition, several new appendices have been added: Appendix B, Using an IRA for Charitable Giving, which is an update of an article that appeared in the March/April 1995 issue of *Probate and Property,* authored by me and published by the American Bar Association Section of Real Property, Probate and Trust Law; Appendix C, Forms, including beneficiary designation forms and trust language forms; and Appendix D, Hypothetical Retirement Plan Scenarios, which illustrates the planning points made in the body of the text.

In preparing the second edition, Thomas C. Foster, an attorney with the firm of Mezzullo & McCandlish who specializes in employee benefits and related issues, reviewed the draft and made many valuable suggestions to improve accuracy and readability. Timothy H. Guare, also an attorney with Mezzullo & McCandlish who specializes in estate planning, also reviewed the draft and made suggestions to improve readability. I am indebted to Edward F. Martin, of New Orleans, Louisiana, for his help in revising the section on community property law considerations. I am also grateful to Maria M. Carnevale, a student of the University of Oregon School of Law, who reviewed the draft for accuracy and checked the endnotes. Finally, my secretary, Andrea D. Tyree, who suffered through innumerable drafts in bringing the first edition to its completion, also was invaluable in completing the second edition. As I mentioned in the preface to the first edition, despite all this assistance, I remain the only guilty party for any errors or omissions (and would appreciate hearing about them from the reader).

Louis A. Mezzullo
October 1997

Preface and Acknowledgments to the First Edition

This monograph is designed for the non-ERISA specialist who engages in estate planning on a somewhat regular basis. Therefore, more knowledge in estate planning than in employee benefits was assumed in its preparation. Every attempt was made to tie the discussion to estate planning practices. While the law in this area is in dire need of reform, little attention was given to proposed changes in the law or regulations, since this work is designed as a guide to the law as it now exists. There are at least two exceptions. First, there is a brief discussion concerning the suggested changes in the requirements under the minimum distribution rules that must be satisfied by a trust in order to qualify as a designated beneficiary. Second, the current ruling position of the Internal Revenue Service ("IRS") with respect to qualifying plan benefits and IRAs for the marital deduction is questioned.

It is hoped that this monograph will permit the non-ERISA specialist to have more confidence when discussing qualified retirement plan benefits and IRAs with his or her clients. Although prepared for the Real Property, Probate and Trust Law Section of the American Bar Association, it is designed to be used by trust officers, financial planners, certified public accountants, insurance professionals, and others, as well as lawyers. The reader is advised to check the current status of the law before advising a client, since the rate of change in this area is rapid. For example, legislation has been proposed to eliminate special averaging and to liberalize the rollover rules.

The origin of this monograph is an outline I prepared for a presentation at the University of Richmond Annual Estate Planning Seminar for Professionals in 1987. Since that time, the outline has been considerably expanded and continually updated. The outline has served as the basis for a chapter in a book I am writing on Planning for the Elderly, to be published in the near future by Callaghan & Company. A draft of this chapter served as a starting point for a study published by the American College of Trust and Estate Counsel entitled "Handbook on Planning for Distributions from Qualified Retirement Plans and Individual Retirement Accounts." The study was the work of the Committee on Employee Benefits in Estate Planning, of which I was and am currently the Chair. The other members of the Committee at the time the original study was prepared were: Richard R. Burns, Allen D. Evans, Thomas H. Foye, E. James Gamble, Mervyn Gerson, C. Wells Hall, III, Morton A. Harris,

Paul Gordon Hoffman, Robert H. Holmes, Marcia Chadwick Holt, John L. Hopwood, Loren C. Ipsen, Edward F. Martin, Raymond W. Rawlings, Cecil A. Ray, Jr., Michael L. Stark, and Charles C. Webb. I gratefully acknowledge the valuable contribution that they made to my knowledge of the area. In particular, the section on community property law considerations is based on a draft of a new section to be added to the study prepared by Edward F. Martin, with the assistance of Edward V. Brennan.

In addition, Robert E. Lee and Jerome L. Lonnes, two members of my firm, made many valuable suggestions to improve the readability of the work. Michael C. Roach, also an attorney with my firm, assisted in research and in locating hard-to-find references. Mary M. Thrower, a summer associate with my firm, checked the references and made valuable suggestions to improve readability. Julie M. Schucht, a legal assistant with my firm, read the final draft and made a number of valuable suggestions. My firm also assisted the monograph by its understanding of my recent deficiency in billable hours. Finally, my secretary, Andrea D. Tyree, suffered through innumerable drafts in bringing this work to its completion. Despite all this assistance, I remain the only guilty party for any errors or omissions (and would appreciate hearing about them from the reader).

Louis A. Mezzullo
June 1991

Chapter One

Introduction

A. Scope of Monograph

This monograph covers planning considerations with respect to distributions from qualified retirement plans and individual retirement accounts (IRAs). For purposes of this monograph, the term *qualified retirement plan* includes tax-deferred annuities for employees of certain tax-exempt organizations and public school systems. Qualified retirement plans are plans that receive favorable tax benefits because they satisfy certain requirements of the Internal Revenue Code (the Code). IRAs also receive favorable tax treatment. The monograph does not deal with distributions from nonqualified retirement plans or deferred compensation plans, including so-called rabbi and secular trusts, nor with Education IRAs that were added by the Taxpayer Relief Act of 1997. Further, this monograph does not deal with decisions about participation in, or contributions to, qualified retirement plans or IRAs, including decisions about whether to roll over or convert balances from a traditional IRA to a Roth IRA.

Income and transfer tax issues are covered in detail. In addition, the rights of a nonparticipant spouse to certain benefits under the participant's qualified retirement plan are explained. Estate and trust administration issues are noted where appropriate. Finally, practical and planning suggestions are provided. Investment and financial planning issues are not addressed.

B. Importance of Subject Matter for Estate Planners

Although most estate planners do not draft qualified retirement plans on a regular basis, they should be aware of the various tax and nontax considerations affecting distributions from qualified retirement plans and IRAs. Benefits from such plans represent a significant portion of the net worth of many clients. In fact, qualified retirement plan benefits, IRAs, and life insurance proceeds may constitute as much as 75 to 80 percent of the intangible wealth of most middle-class Americans.

Unfortunately, properly advising clients with respect to distributions from qualified retirement plans and IRAs involves many complex issues.

Congress has tinkered with the provisions of the Code dealing with the taxation of distributions in almost every major tax act since the adoption of the Employee Retirement Income Security Act of 1974 (ERISA).[1] These changes have continued to accelerate in the years since enactment.

Planning for distributions is also complex because distributions may take many forms, such as lump sum distributions, annuities, installment payments over a fixed period, and distributions qualifying for rollover treatment. Because the identity of the beneficiary can have significant tax and nontax consequences, careful planning is required when designating the beneficiaries who will take any benefits remaining at the death of the participant. When to begin to receive the benefits and over what period they should be paid are decisions that involve many difficult and often competing financial and tax considerations.

These issues must be considered on at least five different occasions for each participant. First, when the participant becomes eligible to participate in a qualified retirement plan or opens an IRA, the participant must select the beneficiary or beneficiaries to take any death benefits payable under the plan or the balance in the IRA account at death (although that selection may usually be changed by the participant at any time up to his or her death, subject to consent rights of his or her spouse). In some cases, the participant must also initially choose a form of payment (although the selection of the form of payment under a qualified retirement plan must be revocable until just before retirement). Second, if the participant is getting a divorce, he or she must ensure that any plan benefits payable to a former spouse are specified in a qualified domestic relations order (QDRO) to avoid being taxed on the amount paid to the former spouse. Third, before the participant retires, the participant must select the form of payment, the period over which the payment will be made, and the beneficiary of any remaining benefits at his or her death. Fourth, after the death of the participant, whether before or after retirement, the personal representative of the deceased participant must determine who is the proper beneficiary or beneficiaries of the decedent's benefits. In many cases, the beneficiary will be free to select the form of benefit. The personal representative or beneficiary must also consider whether a disclaimer of the benefits produces better tax and nontax results. Also, the source of payment of estate, generation-skipping, and income taxes must be factored into the

---

[1] The Employee Retirement Income Security Act of 1974, as amended (ERISA), Pub. L. No. 93-406, 88 Stat. 829.

planning process. Fifth, the participant should consider a Roth IRA rollover any time he or she would qualify for such a rollover.

In making these decisions with respect to qualified retirement plan benefits and IRAs, the participant, beneficiary, or planner must consider a number of factors. First, and perhaps most importantly, the financial needs of the retired participant or beneficiaries must be taken into account. It is futile to plan to postpone the receipt of benefits to defer the payment of income taxes if the participant needs the benefits to pay for his or her current living expenses.

In addition to the financial needs of the participant or beneficiaries, the health of the participant, the participant's spouse, and other beneficiaries must be taken into account. For example, if the participant is in poor health, an annuity, based on standard mortality assumptions, that terminates at the participant's death should not be selected. On the other hand, if the participant's spouse is in poor health, the participant should not select a joint and survivor annuity. However, if the plan is subject to the survivor annuity rules discussed in Section A of Chapter Five, the spouse must consent to any form of payment other than a qualified joint and survivor annuity.

Because distributions from qualified retirement plans and traditional IRAs will be subject to current income tax except to the extent that the participant has made nondeductible contributions, income tax planning is extremely important. Conversely, all "qualified distributions" from Roth IRAs will not be subject to income tax. In addition, irrevocable beneficiary designations during the participant's lifetime may involve taxable gifts, and qualified retirement plan benefits and IRAs will usually be includible in the participant's federal gross estate for estate tax purposes. A distribution of plan benefits may also be a generation-skipping transfer subject to the GST tax.

C. Tax Benefits of Qualified Retirement Plans and IRAs

Qualified retirement plans receive favorable tax treatment under the Code. First, an employer receives a current deduction for contributions made to the plan, while under a nonqualified deferred compensation plan an employer is not entitled to a deduction for a benefit provided to an employee until the employee must include the value of the benefit in taxable income. Second, the employee does not recognize income when the contributions are made to the plan for his or her benefit, but instead pays tax on the benefits when they are actually distributed. Third, the trust that holds the funds is exempt from federal income tax, unless the trust receives unrelated business income; consequently, the trust fund grows more rapidly than a taxable investment since income taxes do not reduce the income or the realized gains added to the fund each year.

Fourth, when distributions from the plan are made to the participant or the participant's beneficiary, favorable tax treatment may be available. For a person who reached age 50 before January 1, 1986, ten-year averaging and capital gain treatment may be available. In addition, certain distributions qualify for rollover treatment. Rollover treatment permits the recipient of the distribution to place the funds in an IRA, or in some cases another qualified retirement plan, thereby deferring the income tax on the distribution until a later date and retaining the benefits in a tax-exempt fund. The Economic Growth and Tax Relief Reconciliation Act of 2001 (EGTRRA 2001) liberalized the rollover rules.

In 2015, an individual may contribute the lesser of $5,500 or the individual's compensation for the year to a traditional IRA or a Roth IRA (or it can be allocated between the two).[2] The dollar amount is adjusted for inflation in increments of $500.[3] An individual who reached age 50 during the taxable year may make an additional catch-up contribution of $1,000. The catch-up amount is not adjusted for inflation.[4] The dollar limit can be doubled if at least half is contributed to an IRA of a spouse of the individual.[5] No contributions may be made to a traditional IRA in the year in which the individual attains age 70½ or any later year.[6] Once amounts have been contributed to an IRA, the investment return is not currently subject to income tax.

The contributions made to a traditional IRA may be deductible for income tax purposes. If either the participant or the participant's spouse is an active participant in a qualified retirement plan, then the amount deductible is reduced or eliminated once the participant's or couple's adjusted gross income (AGI) exceeds a certain amount.[7]

---

[2] Code §§ 219(b)(1), 408(0)(2), 408A(c)(2).
[3] Code § 219(b).
[4] *Id.*
[5] Code § 219(c).
[6] Code § 219(d)(1).
[7] Code § 219(g)(1).

In 2015, in the case of a single individual who is an active participant in a qualified retirement plan, the deductible amount of the individual's IRA contribution is reduced pro rata as the individual's AGI, determined before the IRA deduction, increases from $61,000 to $71,000.[8] For example, if a single individual who is an active participant in a qualified retirement plan has AGI of $66,000 (before taking into account any deduction for a contribution to an IRA), his or her deduction for an IRA contribution during the year is limited to $2,750, or 50 percent of the $5,500 limit on IRA contributions for an individual. The 50 percent reduction is determined by taking the excess of the individual's AGI over $61,000, which is $5,000, and dividing it by $10,000, the excess of $71,000 over $61,000.

In 2015, in the case of a couple filing a joint return, the reduction of the deductible amount begins at $98,000 of AGI, and the couple may no longer deduct contributions to a traditional IRA once their AGI exceeds $118,000.[9] The phase-out range for a married person filing separately is from $0 to $20,000. A special rule allows a married person who is separated from his or her spouse for the entire year and who files a separate return to be treated as a single person for purposes of determining the amount of deductible contributions he or she can make to a traditional IRA.[10]

There is a $200 de minimis deduction available to an individual whose AGI has not reached the complete phase-out amount; *i.e.,* $71,000 for a single taxpayer and $118,000 for married taxpayers filing a joint return.[11]

In addition, the Tax Relief Act of 1997 (TRA 97) allows a spouse of an active participant to make deductible contributions to a traditional IRA, unless the AGI of the couple exceeds $183,000 in 2015. The amount the spouse may deduct is reduced proportionately after the AGI of the couple reaches $183,000, until it reaches $193,000.[12]

TRA 97 added another type of IRA, known as a Roth IRA.[13] Contributions to a Roth IRA, which could be made only in tax years

---

[8] Code §§ 219(g)(2)(A), (3)(B)(ii).
[9] Code §§ 219(g)(2)(A), (3)(B)(i).
[10] Code § 219(g)(4).
[11] Code § 219(g)(2)(B).
[12] TRA 97 § 301(b), amending Code § 219(g), adding new paragraph (7).
[13] Code § 408A, added by TRA 97 § 302(a).

beginning after December 31, 1997, are not deductible.[14] The annual amount that can be contributed is the same as for a traditional IRA, *i.e.,* in 2015, $5,500 in the case of an individual, or $11,000 in the case of a married couple, provided that the contribution to either spouse's IRA does not exceed $5,500.[15] The same increases in the annual amount that can be contributed to a traditional IRA (discussed earlier) also apply to Roth IRAs. In addition, the amount that can be contributed is reduced by any amounts contributed to a traditional IRA. Contributions to a Roth IRA are permitted after age 70½.[16] Contributions for a year (plus earnings) may be shifted from a traditional IRA to a Roth IRA or vice versa at any time before the tax return due date (including extensions) for that year.[17]

Annual contributions to a Roth IRA are subject to a phase-out similar to the contribution deduction phase-out for a traditional IRA, although that phase-out is not dependent on participation in a qualified retirement plan.[18] For a single taxpayer or head of household, the phase-out in 2015 begins at $116,000 of AGI, and no contribution is permitted once AGI reaches $126,000. For a married couple filing a joint return and certain qualifying widowers, the phase-out begins at $183,000 of AGI, and no deduction is permitted once AGI reaches $193,000. For a married individual filing a separate return, the phase-out begins at $0 of AGI, and no deduction is permitted once AGI reaches $10,000. Excess contributions to a Roth IRA are subject to the 6 percent excess contribution excise tax under Code § 4973(f).

A traditional IRA can be rolled into a Roth IRA. The taxable portion of the IRA will be subject to income tax, but not to the 10 percent additional income tax for premature withdrawals or the 6 percent excess contributions excise tax. In lieu of a rollover, the traditional IRA may be converted to a Roth IRA, with the same tax consequences.

Effective for distributions after December 31, 2007, a distribution from a tax-qualified retirement plan, tax-sheltered annuity, or governmental 457 plan may be rolled over directly from such plan into a Roth IRA. The amount rolled over in excess of any nondeductible contributions made to the plan is included in gross income. After 2009, as a result of the 2005

[14] Code § 408A(c)(1).
[15] Code § 408A(c)(2).
[16] Code § 408A(c)(4).
[17] Code § 408A(d)(6).
[18] Code § 408A(c)(3).

Tax Increase Prevention and Reconciliation Act,[19] which amended § 408A to eliminate the income limits on conversions of traditional IRAs to Roth IRAs (which was AGI of $100,000),[20] any individual, regardless of his or her AGI, may roll over amounts from traditional IRAs and eligible retirement plans to a Roth IRA. As a result of this rule, a participant in a qualified retirement plan or other tax-favored plan will not have to roll over a distribution to a traditional IRA in order to roll the same amount into a Roth IRA. With the elimination of the income limitation after 2009, every individual who is either an account holder of a traditional IRA or a participant in a qualified retirement plan will need to consider whether to convert the existing traditional IRA to a Roth IRA or to roll the qualified retirement plan benefit into a Roth IRA.

The ability to roll a benefit directly from a qualified retirement plan into a Roth IRA not only eliminates a step in achieving a Roth IRA conversion, but may also allow more of the amount rolled over to be treated as after-tax contributions not subject to income tax, thus reducing the tax cost of the rollover. Under the normal rules regarding distributions from IRAs, any distribution, including a rollover, will be treated as a pro rata portion of before-tax and after-tax contributions to all the person's IRAs. Consequently, a participant in a qualified retirement plans who has made substantial after-tax contributions to the plan would want to avoid having the plan benefit aggregated with his or her traditional IRAs if they consist of mostly before-tax contributions. A direct rollover of the qualified plan benefit to a Roth IRA would avoid aggregating the plan benefit with the participant's traditional IRAs in determining the amount of before-tax and after-tax contributions.

Although contributions to a Roth IRA are not deductible for income tax purposes, and an individual recognizes taxable income upon the conversion of a traditional IRA to a Roth IRA or the rollover of a qualified retirement plan benefit to a Roth IRA, earnings on the investments in the Roth IRA and qualified distributions from the Roth IRA more than five years after the first contribution to the Roth IRA are not subject to income tax. In addition, the owner of the Roth IRA is not required to take out minimum distributions once he or she has reached age 70½. If the owner's spouse is the beneficiary of the Roth IRA, the spouse is also not subject to

---

[19] Pub. L. No. 109-222, 120 Stat. 345, § 512(a).

[20] *See* § 408A(c)(3), as amended by 2005 Tax Increase Prevention and Reconciliation Act, Pub. L. No. 109-222, 120 Stat. 345, § 512(a).

the minimum distribution rules after the owner dies. Other beneficiaries, however, are subject to the minimum distribution rules.

As mentioned in the last paragraph, distributions from a Roth IRA are not subject to the minimum distribution rules during the account holder's lifetime.[21] Distributions from a Roth IRA are not included in gross income for federal income tax purposes if they are qualified distributions.[22] A *qualified distribution* is any distribution from a Roth IRA if a five tax-year holding period is fulfilled and the distribution is made after the individual reaches 59½, after the individual's death, or on account of the individual's total and permanent disability, or if it is a qualified first-time homebuyer distribution.[23] If the distribution is attributable to annual Roth IRA contributions, the five tax-year holding period is fulfilled if the individual has maintained any Roth IRA for the preceding five taxable years. If the distribution is attributable to amounts rolled over or converted from a traditional IRA, the five tax-year holding period begins with the year of the rollover or conversion. A first-time homebuyer distribution must be used for the cost of acquiring, constructing, or reconstructing (including usual or reasonable settlement, financing, or other closing costs) the principal residence of the account holder or his or her spouse, or the principal residence of a child, grandchild, or ancestor of the owner or spouse and is subject to a lifetime limitation of $10,000 per individual.[24] Other rules apply in determining whether a distribution is a qualified first-time homebuyer distribution.

If a distribution is made before the five-year period, but would otherwise have been a qualified distribution, it will not be subject to the 10 percent premature withdrawal tax. Nonqualified distributions of non-rolled-over amounts are treated as coming first from contributions, and to that extent will not be subject to either the traditional income tax or the 10 percent tax.[25] However, a distribution from a Roth IRA of an amount rolled over from a traditional IRA within the five-year period beginning with the year of the rollover will be subject to the 10 percent premature withdrawal tax absent an exception, even though the distribution would not be includible in the recipient's gross income.[26]

---

[21] Code § 408A(c)(5).
[22] Code § 408A(d)(1).
[23] Code § 408A(d)(2).
[24] Code §§ 408A(d)(2)(A)(iv), (5), 72(t)(2)(F).
[25] Code § 408A(d)(4)(B).
[26] Code § 408A(d)(3)(F).

Whether an individual should make contributions to a traditional IRA or a Roth IRA and whether the individual should roll over or convert a traditional IRA to a Roth IRA depends on a number of factors, and is outside the scope of this monograph.

D. Types of Qualified Retirement Plans

Planning for distributions from qualified retirement plans is complicated partly because of the many types of plans that are available, each of them having different characteristics that affect the timing and form of the distribution of benefits. The type of plan may also affect the extent of a spouse's rights to the participant's interest in the plan. The following is merely a summary of the types of qualified retirement plans and does not explain the factors an employer should consider in choosing one type of plan over another.

Qualified retirement plans are divided into two major categories: defined benefit plans and defined contribution plans.

1. Defined Benefit Plans

Under a *defined benefit plan*, a participant is promised a specific benefit that is determined under a formula contained in the plan. The formula may provide that a participant is entitled to receive, at the participant's normal retirement age, a percentage of the participant's average compensation over some period of time, multiplied by the participant's number of years of service. For example, a participant may be entitled to a monthly pension equal to 1 percent of his or her average monthly earnings over the consecutive five-year period during which the participant had his or her highest average compensation, multiplied by the participant's number of years of service with the employer. Under such a plan, the participant can depend on receiving the promised monthly payment when he or she retires, assuming that the participant remains a participant in the plan until normal retirement age and the employer continues to fund the plan.

The employer is required to make contributions to fund the benefits provided under the plan. The amount of the contribution is determined actuarially, based on certain assumptions, such as expected rates of return, mortality, and turnover. If the employer fails to fund the plan sufficiently, some or all of the participant's benefit may be guaranteed by the Pension Benefit Guaranty Corporation (PBGC). Since the employer has promised the employee a specific benefit, it is the employer who is subject to the risk that the funds in the plan may not earn an adequate rate of return. On the other hand, it is the employer who benefits if the investments achieve a high rate of return, as future contributions needed to fund the benefits will be reduced.

In a defined benefit plan, a participant is frequently not entitled to receive his or her plan benefits in the form of a lump sum distribution. The sponsoring employer may have at least two good reasons for not permitting lump sum distributions from the plan. First, the employer may be concerned that if a participant elects a lump sum distribution, the participant may spend most of the money soon after receipt, leaving nothing for the participant's retirement years. Second, if a significant number of participants retire in any one year and all want lump sum distributions, the plan may be forced to sell a large portion of its investments at an unfavorable time in the marketplace. In addition, many defined benefit plans do not provide a death benefit other than the survivor annuity to which a participant's spouse may be entitled under the Retirement Equity Act of 1984 (REA).

2. Defined Contribution Plans

Under a *defined contribution plan*, the employer makes contributions to the plan that are allocated to the accounts of the participants, usually based on the participant's compensation. When the participant separates from service, dies, or becomes disabled, or at any other time specified in the plan, the participant is entitled to his or her account balance under the plan. The participant's account balance includes employer contributions, forfeitures from the nonvested portions of the accounts of former participants allocated to his or her account while an active participant in the plan, any contributions made by the participant, and any earnings and gains on these amounts, reduced by any losses or administration expenses allocated to the participant's account. Under most defined contribution plans, a participant is entitled to receive a lump sum distribution of his or her account balance upon retirement. In addition, upon the participant's death before retirement, his or her account balance usually is payable in full to the participant's beneficiary or, if no beneficiary has been designated, to the participant's estate. In a defined contribution plan, the participant bears the risk of poor investment performance of the funds allocated to his or her account, but also enjoys the benefit of a high rate of return on such funds. Some defined contribution plans permit the participant to direct the investment of the funds in his or her account.

There are a number of types of defined contribution plans. The simplest to administer, and the most flexible from an employer standpoint, is a *profit-sharing plan*. Under a profit-sharing plan, each year the employer may contribute as much as 25 percent of the total compensation of all the participants in the plan during the year, or may make no contribution at all. However, a profit-sharing plan that does not have substantial and continuing contributions may be required to fully vest all participants. As in the case of most defined contribution plans, a profit-sharing plan usually provides that the employer's contribution will be allocated to the accounts of the participants based on their compensation.

A *money purchase pension plan* requires the employer to make a specific contribution to the plan each year, usually in an amount equal to a percentage of the compensation of each participant. A *target benefit plan*, which also requires a specific contribution each year, provides for proportionately greater allocations to the accounts of older participants. In a target benefit plan, a specific target benefit is selected and the contribution on behalf of each participant is computed to be sufficient to provide this targeted benefit, based on an assumed rate of return. However, as in the case of all defined contribution plans, at the participant's retirement or other event permitting a distribution, the participant is entitled only to the amount that is actually in the account, regardless of whether that amount is sufficient to provide the targeted benefit. Since the account of an older participant has less time to accumulate funds to provide the targeted benefit, the regulations permit a plan to allocate a proportionately larger percentage of the contribution to the accounts of the older participants than would be allocated in a profit-sharing or money purchase pension plan.[27]

In some cases, depending upon the demographics of the employer, a so-called *new comparability plan* may result in proportionately greater benefits going to the highly compensated employees than under a profit-sharing or money purchase pension plan. Under such a plan, the amount allocated to an employee's account is treated as if it were funding a defined benefit plan for that employee. The retirement benefit that is deemed provided by the contribution to non-highly compensated employees is

[27] Treas. Reg. § 1.401(a)(4)-8(b)(3).

compared with the benefits provided to the highly compensated employees, and as long as the comparability of the benefits meets certain minimum standards, the plan satisfies the nondiscrimination rules.

In the previously popular thrift plans, the participant usually makes nondeductible contributions that may or may not be matched by the employer. For example, a thrift plan may permit a participant to make a nondeductible contribution to the plan of up to 10 percent of the participant's compensation during the year. The employer may then match all or part of the participant's contribution.

Thrift plans have been largely supplanted by another type of defined contribution plan permitting participant contributions, the so-called *401(k) plan* or cash or deferred arrangement. Under such a plan, a participant may elect to have his or her compensation reduced or may elect to forgo a bonus and have the forgone salary or bonus contributed to the plan. Although the forgone salary or bonus will be includible in the participant's gross income for purposes of Social Security taxes and Medicare taxes, it will not be includible in the participant's gross income for income tax purposes.[28] In such a plan the employer may also match part or all of the participant's contribution.

There are also several types of plans that are designed to promote ownership of stock of the sponsoring employer corporation. A *stock bonus plan* is similar to a profit-sharing plan except that it is designed to acquire employer stock.[29] In an *employee stock ownership plan (ESOP)*, the plan may borrow money that it uses to buy stock from the employer or shareholders and pledge the stock acquired as security for the loan.[30] The employer may be a guarantor for a loan.[31] An employer's guarantee of a loan to a plan that is not qualified as an ESOP under the Code and regulations is a prohibited transaction, as would be the plan's pledge of its stock.[32]

An employer may choose to adopt a *simplified employee pension plan (SEP)* to avoid the administrative expense involved in establishing and maintaining a qualified retirement plan. Under such a plan, the

[28] Code § 402(e)(3).
[29] Treas. Reg. § 1.401-1(b)(1)(iii).
[30] Code § 4975(d)(3).
[31] Code § 4975(c).
[32] Code § 4975(e).

participants set up their own IRAs, and the employer makes contributions to these IRAs in much the same manner as the employer would make allocations to the participants' accounts in a profit-sharing plan. Unlike a qualified retirement plan that may have graded vesting, however, the participants are always 100 percent vested in the amount contributed by the employer to the IRA. [33]

Finally, the Small Business Job Protection Act of 1996 added the so-called SIMPLE plan, available to employers of 100 or fewer employees.[34] Contributions of up to $10,000 (as adjusted for inflation) are made to a special IRA account for each employee based on salary deferral elections by each employee. The employee's contribution is generally matched by an employer contribution of up to 3 percent of the employee's compensation. The SIMPLE plan is designed to have even lower administrative expenses than an SEP.

E. Non-Tax Rules Relating to Qualified Retirement Plans

1. *Timing of Benefit Payments*

The timing of the payment of benefits from qualified retirement plans and IRAs is controlled under rules contained in both the Code and ERISA. These rules require a plan to give a participant two rights with respect to the timing of benefit payments. First, these rules require a plan to allow a participant to begin receiving his or her benefits by a certain time. Second, these rules permit a participant to postpone the receipt of benefits until the participant reaches the later of the normal retirement date under the plan or age 62. In addition, the Code requires that distributions commence no later than a certain time and imposes a 50 percent tax on undistributed required distributions. The required distribution rules are dealt with in Chapter Two.

Unless the participant otherwise elects, distributions to a participant must commence no later than 60 days after the close of the plan year in which occurs the latest of:

(1) The date the participant attains the earlier of age 65 or the normal retirement age under the plan;

---

[33] Code §§ 408(a)(4), (k)(1).

[34] Code § 408(p).

(2) The tenth anniversary of plan participation; or

(3) The participant's termination of employment.[35]

A qualified retirement plan may not distribute any portion of a participant's benefit before the later of the attainment of normal retirement age or age 62 without the participant's written consent.[36] For the consent to be valid, the participant must be notified of the material features of the plan's optional forms of benefit payments and of his or her right, if any, to defer the commencement of distributions.[37]

This notice must be given no less than 30 and no more than 90 days before payment of the benefits is scheduled to begin.[38] The participant's written consent may not be required before receipt of the notice and may not be given earlier than 90 days before payment of the benefits is scheduled to begin.[39] If the plan is subject to the survivor annuity rules discussed in Chapter Five, the notice must also describe the rights of the participant's spouse to receive either a survivor annuity or the participant's vested accrued benefit.[40]

Generally, no consent is required if the value of the participant's benefit is $5,000 or less.[41] TRA 2001 provides that a plan may disregard the value of a rollover in determining the value of a participant's benefit.[42] If the plan is subject to the survivor annuity requirements, the cash-out of a benefit with a value of $5,000 or less is not permitted after the participant's annuity starting date, unless the participant and spouse (or if the participant has died, the surviving spouse) consent to the distribution.[43] The participant's annuity starting date is the date regular payments of the participant's benefit are scheduled to begin. Furthermore, a distribution may be made without the consent of the beneficiary after the death of the participant unless the plan is subject to the qualified survivor annuity rules and the beneficiary is the participant's surviving spouse.[44]

---

[35] Code § 401(a)(14); ERISA § 206(a).
[36] Code § 411(a)(11)(A); Treas. Reg. § 1.411(a)-11(c)(4).
[37] Treas. Reg. § 1.411(a)-11(c)(2)(i).
[38] Treas. Reg. § 1.411(a)-11(c)(2)(ii).
[39] *Id.*
[40] Code § 417(a)(3); Treas. Reg. § 1.401(a)-20, Q&A 36.
[41] Code § 411(a)(11)(A).
[42] Code § 411(a)(11)(D), added by TRA 2001 § 648(a)(1).
[43] Code § 417(e)(1).
[44] Treas. Reg. §§ 1.411(a)-11(c)(5), 1.417(e)-1(b)(1).

The Code requires that distributions commence no later than April 1 of the calendar year following the calendar year during which the participant attains age 70½, regardless of whether the participant retires, except for a participant in a qualified retirement plan who does not own more than 5 percent of the sponsoring employer, in which case the payment of benefits can be deferred until April 1 after the year in which the participant retires.[45] This rule is subject to certain exceptions that are discussed in Chapter Two.

Qualified retirement plans may provide for the distribution of benefits upon death, disability, retirement (early, normal, or deferred), separation from service, or plan termination. Distributions from pension plans (defined benefit plans and money purchase pension plans) generally are not permitted before these events.[46] Although money purchase pension plans are defined contribution plans, they are treated as pension plans under the Code with respect to a number of issues, including the prohibition on in-service distributions. *In-service distributions* are distributions made while the participant continues to work for the sponsoring employer. Pension plans may permit distributions to an active participant upon attainment of normal retirement age, and an active participant who reached age 50 before 1986 may elect special averaging for such a distribution if the distribution qualifies as a lump sum distribution, the distribution is received on or after the normal retirement age under the plan, and the participant has reached age 59½.[47] Special averaging and lump sum treatment are discussed in Chapter Three.

Although in-service distributions from pension plans generally are prohibited,[48] the plan may permit a participant to withdraw mandatory employee contributions and the earnings on mandatory employee contributions if he or she ceases plan participation, even if he or she does not terminate employment.[49] *Mandatory contributions* are contributions that are required either as a condition of employment or participation in the plan, or to receive benefits attributable to employer contributions. In addition, a pension plan may permit a participant who continues to

45 Code §§ 401(a)(9)(A), (C).

46 Rev. Rul. 74-254, 1974-1 C.B. 91.

47 Priv. Ltr. Rul. 8926084.

48 Treas. Reg. § 1.401-1(b)(1)(i).

49 Rev. Rul. 60-281, 1960-2 C.B. 146.

participate in the plan to withdraw voluntary nondeductible contributions and the earnings on voluntary nondeductible contributions at any time.[50]

Profit-sharing plans, on the other hand, may provide for distributions after a fixed number of years (at least two), the attainment of a stated age, or upon the prior occurrence of an event such as disability, retirement, death, or severance of employment.[51] Profit-sharing plans may permit hardship distributions while the participant continues to work for the sponsoring employer.

Distributions of elective deferrals from 401(k) plans (amounts that are attributable to employer contributions made pursuant to a participant's salary reduction election) are only permitted when:

(1) A participant separates from service, dies, becomes disabled, or reaches age 59½;[52]

(2) The plan terminates without the establishment or maintenance of another defined contribution plan other than an ESOP, but only if the participant's entire interest is distributed within one taxable year of the participant;[53]

(3) A corporation disposes of substantially all its assets in a trade or business or its interest in a subsidiary to another corporation, but only if:

    (a) The participant continues employment with the purchaser or subsidiary;

    (b) The transferor corporation continues to maintain the plan after the disposition; and

    (c) Distributions of the participant's entire interest are made within one taxable year;[54] or

---

[50] Rev. Rul. 69-277, 1969-1 C.B. 116.
[51] Treas. Reg. § 1.401-1(b)(1)(ii).
[52] Code §§ 401(k)(2)(B)(i)(I), (III).
[53] Code §§ 401(k)(2)(B)(i)(II), 401(k)(10)(A), (B), as added by TAMRA § 1011(k)(1)(B).
[54] Code §§ 401(k)(2)(B)(i)(II), (10)(A), (B).

(4) The participant incurs a hardship (as defined in the regulations).[55]

For plan years beginning after 1988, hardship distributions from 401(k) plans are limited to elective deferrals and may not include any income earned during post-1988 plan years on the elective deferrals.[56] A hardship distribution is not eligible for rollover treatment.[57]

2. *Type of Benefits*

Generally, distributions from qualified retirement plans are made pursuant to the options set forth in the plan document. The options may include a life annuity, a life annuity with a guaranteed number of payments, a joint and survivor annuity, installments, and a lump sum. Under a life annuity, a specific dollar amount is paid to the participant (and under a joint and survivor annuity, to the participant's beneficiary after the participant dies), and at the death of the participant (or the survivor of the participant and the beneficiary) the annuity terminates. A life annuity with a "period certain" feature (such as ten years) provides a specific dollar amount payable each month or year over the life of the participant, and if the participant dies before the end of the period certain, the remaining payments during the period certain will be made to the participant's designated beneficiary. For example, if the participant elects a ten-year certain and life annuity with $1,000 payable each month and the participant dies before the expiration of 120 months, $1,000 will be paid to the participant's designated beneficiary each month during the balance of the 120-month period.

A plan may not condition the availability of an optional form of benefit on the discretion of either the employer or the plan administrator.[58] On the other hand, a plan may condition the availability of an optional form of benefit on objective conditions that are specifically set forth in the plan.[59] For example, a plan may condition a lump sum distribution on the extreme financial hardship of the participant as defined in the plan.[60]

---

[55] Code § 401(k)(2)(B)(i)(IV).
[56] *Id.*; Treas. Reg. § 1.401(k)-1(d)(3)(iii)(B)(6).
[57] Code § 402(c)(4)(C).
[58] Treas. Reg. §§ 1.401(a)-4, Q&A 3, 1.411(d)-4, Q&A 4.
[59] Treas. Reg. § 1.411(d)-4, Q&A 6.
[60] Treas. Reg. § 1.411(d)4, Q&A 6(a)(2).

The minimum distribution rules, discussed in Section C of Chapter Two, limit the distribution period (the period over which the payments are to be made) once the participant reaches his or her required beginning date (RBD).

Under the Code and ERISA, as amended by REA, qualified retirement plan benefits generally must be paid in the form of a qualified joint and survivor annuity, and death benefits must be paid in the form of a qualified preretirement survivor annuity. In both cases, the participant's spouse must be named as the beneficiary of the survivor annuity.[61] The spouse may consent to a waiver of either or both survivor annuities. These rules are discussed in detail in Chapter Five. A profit-sharing or stock bonus plan generally is not required to provide the survivor annuities if certain requirements are satisfied, including the requirement that at the participant's death the participant's vested accrued benefit be paid to the participant's surviving spouse unless the surviving spouse has consented to the designation of another beneficiary.[62]

3. *Determination of Qualified Retirement Plan Benefits*

A. Accrual of Benefits

A participant's *accrued benefit* under a defined benefit plan is the actuarial value of the participant's normal retirement benefit that would be payable at the participant's normal retirement date, determined in accordance with the plan formula and benefit accrual rules.[63] The actuarial assumptions and interest rates that are used in calculating the value of the accrued benefit must be set forth in the plan.[64]

The most common method of determining the portion of the participant's normal retirement benefit that has accrued at any given time is the fractional method. Under the fractional method, the participant's years of participation at the time the accrued benefit is being calculated are compared to the total years of participation the participant would have if the participant continued to participate in the plan until the participant's normal retirement age.

---

[61] Code § 401(a)(11)(A); ERISA § 205; REA §§ 103(a), 203(a).
[62] Code § 401(a)(11)(B)(iii).
[63] Code § 411(a)(7)(A)(i).
[64] Code § 401(a)(25).

For example, assume that a participant commences participating in a plan at age 35, the plan has a normal retirement age of 65, and the participant separates from service at age 40. The participant's accrued benefit is one-sixth of his or her normal retirement benefit, determined by comparing the number of years of participation that the participant has at age 40, five years, with the total number of years the participant would have at the participant's normal retirement age, 30 years.

If the participant's normal retirement benefit under the plan formula payable at the participant's normal retirement age is determined to be $3,000 a month, the participant's accrued benefit at age 40 is one-sixth of this amount or $500 a month. If the participant is entitled to elect a lump sum distribution at the time the participant separates from service at age 40, the participant will be entitled to the actuarial equivalent of the value of $500 a month payable at age 65. The actual lump sum amount will be considerably discounted from its value at the participant's normal retirement date, because the plan has 25 fewer years to invest the employer contributions to fund the participant's accrued benefit.

In a defined contribution plan, the participant's accrued benefit is the participant's account balance, which is the sum of employer contributions and forfeitures from the nonvested portions of the accounts of former participants allocated to his or her account, any employee contributions, and earnings and gains on those amounts less any losses and administration expenses deducted from those amounts.[65]

A participant's accrued benefit may not be decreased by a plan amendment[66] and benefit accruals may not cease because a participant has reached a certain age.[67] A *top-heavy plan*, which is a plan that disproportionately benefits certain key employees, such as officers and major shareholders, must provide a minimum benefit to non-key employees.[68]

B. VESTING OF BENEFITS

A participant is only entitled to the vested portion of the accrued benefit, which may be only a fraction of the benefit. The participant must always

---

[65] Code § 411(a)(7)(A)(ii).
[66] Code § 411(d)(6).
[67] Code §§ 411(b)(1)(H), (2)(A).
[68] Code § 416(c).

be 100 percent vested in the balances attributable to his or her own contributions to the plan and elective deferrals under a 401(k) plan.[69] In addition, a participant must be 100 percent vested in any benefits attributable to employer contributions when he or she reaches normal retirement age or upon termination or partial termination of a plan or complete discontinuance of contributions to a profit-sharing plan or a stock bonus plan.[70]

A plan may provide that a participant's vested interest in employer contributions, forfeitures, and earnings on these amounts depends upon the years of service the participant has with the employer at any given time.[71] For example, a participant in a defined benefit plan may be entitled to no vested interest in his or her accrued benefit attributable to employer contributions and forfeitures until the participant has completed five years of service with the sponsoring employer, when the participant must be 100 percent vested. This type of vesting is referred to as *cliff vesting*. However, a defined benefit plan may instead adopt a graded vesting schedule under which the participant must be entitled to at least a 20 percent vested interest in his or her accrued benefit after three years of service, and an additional 20 percent for each year of service until the participant has seven years of service, when he or she must be 100 percent vested in his or her accrued benefit.

A defined contribution plan may provide that a participant is not entitled to any vested interest in his or her accrued benefit attributable to employer contributions and forfeitures until the participant has completed three years of service with the sponsoring employer, when he or she must be 100 percent vested. On the other hand, a defined contribution plan may adopt a graded vesting schedule under which the participant must be entitled to at least a 20 percent vested interest in his or her accrued benefit after two years of service, and an additional 20 percent for each year of service until the participant has six years of service, when he or she must be 100 percent vested in his or her accrued benefit.[72] If a plan requires two years of service before a participant is eligible to participate in the plan, the participant must be 100 percent vested in his or her accrued benefit when he or she becomes a participant in the plan.[73]

---

[69] Code §§ 411(a)(1), 401(k)(2)(C).
[70] Code §§ 411(a), (d)(3).
[71] Code § 411(a)(2)(A).
[72] Code § 411(a)(2)(B).
[73] Code § 410(a)(1)(B)(i).

More rapid vesting is required in a top-heavy plan. Under a cliff vesting schedule, 100 percent vesting must occur after three years of service. Under graded vesting, a participant must be at least 20 percent vested in his or her accrued benefit after two years of service, with an additional 20 percent required for each year of service until the participant has six years of service, when he or she must be 100 percent vested in his or her accrued benefit.[74] TRA 2001 applies the top-heavy vesting schedules to matching employer contributions for plan years beginning after 2001.[75]

[74] Code § 416(b).

[75] Code § 411(a)(12), added by TRA 2001 §§ 633(a)(1), (2).

Chapter Two

Penalty Taxes

A. Introduction

Because of the favorable tax benefits afforded to qualified retirement plans and IRAs, Congress enacted three rather complex penalty taxes to ensure that participants in qualified retirement plans and IRAs do not use the tax benefits for any purpose other than to provide for retirement income, unless the other purposes are merely incidental to the provision of retirement income.

The first of these taxes penalizes a participant who wishes to withdraw his or her benefits before retirement. A 10 percent additional income tax is imposed on withdrawals that a participant makes from a qualified retirement plan or an IRA before reaching age 59½ unless one of the exceptions discussed in Section B of this chapter applies.

The second penalty forces a participant in a qualified retirement plan or a traditional IRA to begin taking his or her benefits after dying or reaching age 70½ (or, in some cases, after he or she retires), preventing the participant from leaving the benefit in the plan to continue to accumulate tax-free income indefinitely. These requirements do not apply to Roth IRA balances prior to the participant's death. A 50 percent tax is imposed on the excess of the amount of the benefit required to be distributed during the year over the amount actually distributed.

The third penalty was a 15 percent excise tax that was imposed on excess retirement distributions and excess retirement accumulations, which were amounts in excess of certain threshold amounts. The 15 percent tax was designed to penalize those participants who had avoided the limitations that apply to the amount of benefits that can be provided under qualified retirement plans, usually by participating in plans of more than one employer at the same time. The tax also had the effect of penalizing those participants who had achieved extraordinarily high investment returns under defined contribution plans and IRAs. The Small Business Act suspended the excise tax on excess retirement distributions during lifetime for distributions received in 1997, 1998, and 1999. TRA 97 repealed the 15 percent tax, effective for distributions and decedents dying after 1996.

In planning to avoid one or more of these penalty taxes, several points should be considered. First, with respect to the 10 percent tax on premature distributions, it should be recognized that if a participant needs the plan benefits for his or her support and maintenance, the participant usually will be in a rather low income tax bracket. In such a case, the 10 percent penalty should not deter the participant from taking the money out of the plan or IRA if he or she really needs it. In addition, if the amounts have been held in a qualified retirement plan or IRA for more than a few years, the benefit of the tax-free accumulation of the earnings in the plan or IRA usually will more than offset the 10 percent penalty on the distribution. Put another way, even if the participant knows he or she will need to withdraw the amount before 59½, making contributions to the plan or IRA still yields tax benefits.

On the other hand, the 50 percent penalty on required distributions not actually distributed should always be avoided, since the 50 percent tax will outweigh any benefit gained by deferring the receipt of taxable income.

B. Premature Distributions

The Code discourages the early withdrawal of benefits by imposing a penalty in the form of an additional 10 percent income tax on the taxable portion of a distribution from a qualified retirement plan or IRA before the participant reaches age 59½, unless an exception applies.[76] The rate of the tax is increased to 25 percent if the early withdrawal is from a simple retirement account (SRA) during the two-year period beginning on the date the employee's participation in the SRA began.[77] SRAs, which were created by the Small Business Act, are employer-sponsored retirement plans using individual IRAs.

A distribution made to a beneficiary or to the estate of a participant after the death of the participant is not subject to the penalty,[78] nor is a distribution because of the participant's total disability subject to the penalty.[79] Because of the disability exception, a participant may plan on using qualified retirement plan benefits and IRAs to supplement his or her income should he or she become totally disabled before age 59½.

[76] Code § 72(t).
[77] Code § 72(t)(6).
[78] Code § 72(t)(2)(A)(ii).
[79] Code § 72(t)(2)(A)(iii).

Certain kinds of distributions are excepted because the penalty is imposed only on the portion of a distribution included in income. Accordingly, the tax does not apply to a distribution that is rolled into an IRA or a qualified plan or to the portion of a distribution that represents the participant's basis in the plan.[80] A participant's basis in the plan will usually consist of nondeductible employee contributions and amounts that have been taxed to the participant because of life insurance coverage provided by insurance policies owned by the plan. The participant's basis in the plan is explained more fully in Section B of Chapter Three. The costs that are taxed to a participant because of life insurance coverage provided by a plan also are not subject to the 10 percent penalty.[81]

A distribution from a qualified retirement plan to a spouse or former spouse who is an alternate payee under a qualified domestic relations order (QDRO) is not subject to the 10 percent penalty, since the distribution is taxable to the alternate payee rather than the participant.[82] This exception does not apply to a distribution from an IRA, as an IRA is not subject to a QDRO.[83] However, the transfer of an individual's interest in an IRA to his or her spouse or former spouse under a divorce or separation instrument is a nontaxable transfer under Code § 408(d)(6).

The 10 percent penalty does not apply to distributions of excess deferrals, excess contributions, and excess aggregate contributions.[84] These are amounts that are returned to the participant to avoid certain penalties that apply to either a plan or a participant in a plan that permits elective deferrals (salary reductions contributed to a 401(k) plan) or nondeductible employee contributions or employer matching contributions. *Excess deferrals* are amounts deferred in excess of the dollar limit applicable to 401(k) plans. *Excess contributions* and *excess aggregate contributions* are either salary reduction amounts contributed to a 401(k) plan or the total of nondeductible employee contributions plus employer matching contributions that exceed the permissible amounts under the nondiscrimination rules applicable to such contributions.

---

[80] Code § 72(t)(1).
[81] IRS Notice 89-25, 1989-1 C.B. 662, Q&A 11.
[82] Code § 72(t)(2)(C).
[83] Code § 72(t)(3)(A).
[84] Code §§ 401(k)(8)(D), (m)(7)(A), 402(g)(2)(C).

The 10 percent penalty does not apply to dividends paid to a participant with respect to certain qualifying employer securities held by an ESOP.[85]

An infrequently used exception excludes distributions during a year to a participant to the extent that the participant is entitled to a deduction for medical expenses paid during the year, whether or not the participant actually itemizes his or her deductions.[86] Currently, an individual may deduct medical expenses to the extent that the amount of medical expenses paid during the year exceeds 10 percent of the individual's AGI. A distribution qualifying for this exception is still includible in the participant's gross income.

There is an additional exception for withdrawals from an IRA used by the participant to pay for medical insurance for the participant and the participant's spouse and dependents if the participant has received unemployment compensation for 12 consecutive weeks under any federal or state unemployment compensation law. The exception applies for the taxable year in which the unemployment compensation is paid or in the succeeding taxable year. The exception no longer applies after the participant has been employed for at least 60 days after the period of unemployment. The exception also applies to self-employed individuals who are not eligible for unemployment compensation under applicable law, but would have received unemployment compensation for at least 12 weeks but for the fact that the individual was self-employed.[87]

Two additional exceptions from the 10 percent penalty apply to distributions from an IRA. The first exception applies to distributions from an IRA for qualified higher education expenses for the taxpayer, the taxpayer's spouse, or any child or grandchild of the taxpayer or the taxpayer's spouse.[88] The second exception, which also is one of the allowable purposes for a qualified distribution (nontaxable) from a Roth IRA, applies to qualified first-time homebuyer distributions, which are distributions used for the cost of acquiring, constructing, or reconstructing (including usual or reasonable settlement, financing, or other closing costs) the principal residence of the account holder or his or her spouse, or the principal residence of a child, grandchild, or ancestor of the account holder or spouse.[89]

---

[85] Code § 72(t)(2)(A)(vi).

[86] Code § 72(t)(2)(B).

[87] Code § 72(t)(2)(D).

[88] Code §§ 72(t)(2)(E), § 72(t)(7).

[89] Code §§ 72(t)(2)(F), 72(t)(8).

The most important exceptions to the 10 percent or 25 percent penalty are the exception for substantially equal periodic payments[90] and the exception for payments made to a participant who separates from service after reaching age 55.[91] The exception for payments after separation from service after age 55 applies only to distributions from qualified retirement plans, not IRAs.[92] The exception does not apply unless the separation from service occurs after reaching age 55.[93] If the participant separates from service at age 54, a distribution after reaching age 55 will not be exempt from the 10 percent penalty under this exception.

The substantially equal periodic payment exception applies to a distribution from a qualified retirement plan only if the participant has separated from the service of the sponsoring employer, while the exception applies to a distribution from an IRA regardless of whether the IRA owner has retired.[94] If a participant needs to reach his or her benefits under a qualified retirement plan maintained by the participant's current employer but does not want to quit his or her job, the participant might be able to take a distribution from the plan that qualifies for rollover treatment[95] and roll it into an IRA. The participant may then begin to receive distributions from the IRA under the substantially equal periodic payment exception.

To satisfy the substantially equal periodic payment exception, substantially equal payments of the plan benefit or IRA must be made at least annually over the life of the participant or the joint lives of the participant and his or her designated beneficiary, or over a period certain equal to the life expectancy of the participant or the joint life expectancies of the participant and his or her designated beneficiary.[96] The beneficiary whose life is being used to determine the payout period must be the same person entitled to any benefits remaining at the participant's death.[97]

---

[90] Code § 72(t)(2)(A)(iv).
[91] Code § 72(t)(2)(A)(v).
[92] Code § 72(t)(3)(A).
[93] Ann. 87-2, 1987-12 I.R.B. 38, Q&A A-3(3).
[94] Code § 72(t)(3)(B).
[95] *See* Chapter Three, Section H.
[96] Code § 72(t)(2)(A)(iv). The IRS has approved three methods of determining whether the substantially equal periodic payment requirement has been satisfied. IRS Notice 89-25, 1981-1 C.B. 662, Q&A 12. The advisor may want to compare the annual payment under all three methods to determine the most suitable method for the participant's needs. *See* Toolson, "Structuring Substantially Equal Payments to Avoid the Premature Withdrawal Penalty," 73 *J. Taxation* 276 (Nov. 1990), for a discussion of these methods.
[97] Code § 72(t)(2)(A)(iv).

Once the exception for substantially equal periodic payments applies, any modification of the series of payments for a reason other than the death or disability of the participant will require the participant to pay the penalties, plus interest on the penalties, that would have been imposed on the distributions had the exception not applied to any of the payments.[98] This recapture rule will not apply if the modification occurs after the later of the end of the five-year period beginning with the date of the first payment or the date the participant reaches age 59½. For example, if the participant begins receiving substantially equal periodic payments under this exception when the participant is age 53, the participant may not modify the series of payments until reaching age 59½, which is more than five years after the payments commenced. On the other hand, if the participant begins receiving substantially equal periodic payments under this exception when he or she is age 58, the participant must wait until reaching age 63 to change the series of payments. In the latter case, only the payments made before the participant reached age 59½ are subject to the recapture of penalties and interest.

Two transition rules may enable a participant to avoid the 10 percent penalty. Under the first transition rule, the penalty does not apply to a participant, other than a five percent owner, who separated from service before March 1, 1986, and who was receiving benefits as of that date.[99] A *five percent owner* is a participant who is a sole proprietor, or who owns more than 5 percent of the stock of the sponsoring employer or more than 5 percent of the partnership interests of a sponsoring partnership. A five percent owner was subject to a 10 percent penalty on premature distributions before TRA 86 imposed such a penalty on all participants.

The 10 percent penalty also does not apply if the benefits are being paid pursuant to a written designation of the form of benefit that was signed by the participant before January 1, 1984, and that satisfied the transition rule under TEFRA § 242(b)(2).[100] Since the transition rule is used primarily to avoid the 50 percent tax on required distributions, it is discussed in detail in the next section of this chapter.

---

[98] Code § 72(t)(4)(A).

[99] TRA 86 § 1123(e)(3).

[100] TRA 86 § 1123(e)(4); IRS Notice 83-23, 1983-2 C.B. 418.

The 10 percent penalty does not apply to distributions made after December 31, 1999, on account of an IRS levy under § 6331 on a qualified retirement plan.[101]

C. Minimum Distribution Requirements

1. Introduction

On April 17, 2002, the Treasury published final regulations dealing with the required minimum distribution rules that apply to benefits held in defined contribution qualified retirement plans, individual retirement accounts (IRAs), and certain other deferred compensation arrangements. Final regulations were issued on June 15, 2004, dealing with defined benefit plans and annuity contracts.[102]

Section 401(a)(9) requires that plan benefits be distributed to participants and their beneficiaries over certain periods to prevent the indefinite deferral of the federal income tax on the income accumulated in the plan and to ensure that the favorable tax treatment afforded to qualified retirement plans serves the intent of Congress to encourage saving for retirement. Section 4974 imposes a 50 percent excise tax on the amount of a required minimum distribution that is not distributed to a participant or beneficiary within a particular year. Sections 408(a)(6) and 408(b)(3) apply these minimum distribution rules to IRAs and individual retirement annuities (both referred to in this monograph as IRAs). Section 457(d)(2) applies these rules to certain deferred compensation plans for tax-exempt organizations or state and local government employees. Generally, by a participant's required beginning date, either the entire plan benefit or IRA must be distributed to the participant or the distribution of the plan benefit or IRA must commence and be made over one of the following periods: (1) the life of the participant; (2) the joint lives of the participant and a designated beneficiary; (3) a period not extending beyond the life expectancy of the participant; or (4) a period not extending beyond the joint and last survivor expectancy of the participant and a designated beneficiary.[103] If the participant dies before the entire plan benefit or IRA has been distributed, the beneficiary must receive the balance over a

---

[101] Code § 72(t)(2)(A)(vii); Pub. L. No. 105-206, § 3436(a).
[102] Treas. Reg. § 1.401(a)(9)-6.
[103] Code § 401(a)(9)(A).

certain period of time specified in the Code.[104] The regulations substantially modify the statutory periods specified in the Code.

Distributions may be made in a manner that does not satisfy the minimum distribution rules if the form of benefit and the beneficiary were designated in writing before January 1, 1984, under the transition rule added by § 242(b)(2) of TEFRA.[105] The form of payment and beneficiary designation must satisfy the law in effect before January 1, 1984, including the incidental death benefit rule.[106] It should be determined whether such a written election exists when planning for a person who was a participant in a plan before January 1, 1984.[107] If the form of payment is changed or the payout period is increased, the transition rule will no longer apply.[108] Securing a spouse's consent to payment in the form specified in the TEFRA § 242(b)(2) election, which may be required as a waiver of a qualified preretirement survivor annuity or a qualified joint and survivor annuity, does not invalidate the application of the transition rule.[109] The transition rule no longer applies if the benefits covered by that rule are transferred to another plan by the voluntary action of the participant.[110] Once the transition rule no longer applies, the new minimum distribution rules apply and may require a substantial distribution in the first year in order to catch up.[111]

---

[104] Code § 401(a)(9)(B).

[105] *See* IRS Notice 83-23, 1983-2 C.B. 418, and Pub. L. No. 99-514, § 1121(d)(4)(A).

[106] *See* II, C, 3, b, below, for a discussion of the incidental death benefit rule.

[107] *See* Priv. Ltr. Rul. 9638040 (decedent's failure to name beneficiary under TEFRA § 242(b) election requires distribution of his interest in plan under § 401(a)(9) without regard to such election). *See also* Priv. Ltr. Rul. 199908060, wherein the IRS ruled that the beneficiary designation did not satisfy the requirements of TEFRA § 242(b)(2), and IRS Notice 83-23 because the designation provided only for payments to a beneficiary rather than to the participant and a beneficiary, the method of distribution conflicted with the plan provisions for paying benefits, a distribution delayed until after the death of the surviving spouse failed to provide for incidental death benefits, the distribution start date was not specified, and the period over which benefits were to be paid was not specified. Thus, the § 401(a)(9) distribution rules governed without regard to the decedent's election under TEFRA.

[108] *See* Priv. Ltr. Rul. 9617048 (TEFRA § 242(b)(2) election revoked by 1990 execution of forms changing time distributions were to commence from normal retirement age (65) to age 70½).

[109] Treas. Reg. § 1.401(a)(9)-8, Q&A-13; 1987 Prop. Treas. Reg. § 1.401(a)(9)-1, Q&A J-1; 2001 Prop. Treas. Reg. § 1.401(a)(9)-8, Q&A-13.

[110] Treas. Reg. § 1.401(a)(9)-8, Q&A-14, -15; 1987 Prop. Treas. Reg. § 1.401(a)(9)-1, Q&A J-2; 2001 Prop. Treas. Reg. § 1.401(a)(9)-8, Q&A-14, -15.

[111] Treas. Reg. § 1.401(a)(9)-8, Q&A-14, -15; 1987 Prop. Treas. Reg. § 1.401(a)(9)-1, Q&A J-4; 2001 Prop. Treas. Reg. § 1.401(a)(9)-8, Q&A-14, -15.

The following discussion focuses on the rules that apply to individual retirement arrangements, which include defined contribution plans, such as profit-sharing plans, 401(k) plans (also referred to as cash or deferred plans), money purchase pension plans, IRAs, 403(b) plans, and 457 plans.

2. Required Beginning Date

The required beginning date (RBD) for traditional IRA account holders and participants in a qualified retirement plan who own more than 5 percent of the sponsoring employer (*i.e.*, a sole proprietor, or a partner, limited liability company member, or shareholder who owns more than 5 percent of the sponsoring employer) is April 1 following the calendar year in which the individual reaches age 70½.[112] The RBD for participants in qualified retirement plans who do not own more than 5 percent of the sponsoring employer is April 1 following the later of the calendar year in which the participant reaches age 70½ or the calendar year in which the participant retires.[113] Note that if the participant waits to receive his or her first RBD until April 1 of the year following the year in which he or she reaches age 70½ (or retires), he or she must receive another RBD before the end of the same year.

The final regulations permit a qualified retirement plan to mandate that the RBD for all employees is April 1 after the calendar year in which the participant reaches age 70½, regardless of whether he or she has retired.[114] If a participant who does not own more than 5 percent of the sponsoring employer receives a distribution before he or she retires, the participant may roll the distribution into his or her own IRA within 60 days of receipt, but will then become subject to the minimum distribution rules applicable to the IRA.

---

[112] Treas. Reg. §§ 1.401(a)(9)-2, A-2(b) and 1.408-8, A-3.
[113] Treas. Reg. § 1.401(a)(9)-2, A-2(a).
[114] Treas. Reg. § 1.401(a)(9)-2, A-2(e) and A-6(b).

3. *Distributions During Participant's Lifetime*

The final regulations greatly simplified the method of determining the required minimum distributions during a participant's lifetime. While the participant is alive, the minimum distribution is determined annually by dividing the applicable distribution period into the value of the participant's plan benefits and IRAs as of the valuation date (December 31 in the case of an IRA) in the year preceding the year in which the distribution has to be made.[115] For purposes of determining the value of a participant's account, distributions after the end of the calendar year are disregarded and contributions after the end of the year may be disregarded.[116] Consequently, a distribution made before a participant's RBD, but after the year in which the participant reaches age 70½ (or retires, in the case of a participant in a qualified retirement plan who does not own more than 5 percent of the sponsoring employer), will not reduce the value of the plan benefit or IRA for purposes of determining the required minimum distribution for the participant's second distribution year that must be made by December 31 of the year in which the RBD occurs. On the other hand, a contribution to a defined contribution plan that is allocated to a participant's account as of a date in the preceding calendar year does not have to be added to the value of the participant's account for purposes of determining the required minimum distribution for the year in which the contribution was made.

For purposes of determining the minimum distribution for a particular distribution calendar year, the account balance is not reduced by distributions made pursuant to a QDRO after the end of the valuation year.[117]

Generally, the applicable distribution period is determined using the uniform lifetime table in Reg. § 1.401(a)(9)-9, A-2, which is based on the participant's age and the age of an individual ten years younger than the participant in each distribution calendar year.[118] That table is set out in Appendix A. The final regulations included life expectancy tables for determining the applicable distribution period, using the basic 2000 individual annuity mortality table projected to 2003.[119]

---

[115] Treas. Reg. § 1.401(a)(9)-5, A-1(a).
[116] Treas. Reg. § 1.401(a)(9)-5, A-3.
[117] Priv. Ltr. Rul. 9011031.
[118] Treas. Reg. § 1.401(a)(9)-5, A-4.
[119] Treas. Reg. § 1.401(a)(9)-9.

If the sole designated beneficiary is the employee's surviving spouse at all times during the year and the spouse is more than ten years younger than the participant, the applicable distribution period is the joint and last survivor expectancy of the participant and spouse, using their ages in each distribution calendar year.[120] This joint and last survivor expectancy is determined pursuant to Reg. § 1.401(a)(9)-9, A-3. Appendix C contains the multiples for participants age 70 to 80 with spouses age 45 to 49.[121]

The surviving spouse will be treated as the participant's sole designated beneficiary if he or she is the outright beneficiary of the participant's entire plan benefit or IRA or a separate share thereof. If the plan benefit or IRA is payable to a trust and the surviving spouse is a beneficiary of the trust, he or she will be treated as the participant's sole designated beneficiary only if the trust agreement provides that entire required minimum distribution and any other distributions from the plan or IRA that are paid to the trust each year are redistributed to the surviving spouse; in other words, no distributions from the plan or IRA made during the surviving spouse's lifetime will be held in the trust for eventual distribution to remainder beneficiaries.[122] Because marriage is determined as of January 1 of each year, death or divorce during the year will not change the applicable distribution period until the following calendar year.[123] However, if the participant, after a divorce, changes the beneficiary during the same calendar year, then the new beneficiary would be taken into account in determining the applicable distribution period for that year. If the spouse is no longer the participant's designated beneficiary for any reason other than death or divorce before the end of a particular calendar year, the participant must use the uniform lifetime table for purposes of determining the applicable distribution period in that year.

The minimum distribution incidental benefit (MDIB) rule mandated by the Code[124] is deemed to be satisfied if distributions are made pursuant to the uniform lifetime table or, in the case of a spouse more than ten years younger than the participant, are based on the joint and last survivor expectancy of the participant and the spouse determined each year.[125]

---

[120] Treas. Reg. § 1.401(a)(9)-5, A-4(b).

[121] Treas. Reg. § 1.401(a)(9)-5, A-6.

[122] Treas. Reg. § 1.401(a)(9)-5, A-7(c)(3), *Example 1*.

[123] Treas. Reg. § 1.401(a)(9)-5, A-4(b)(2).

[124] Code § 401(a)(9)(G).

[125] Treas. Reg. § 1.401(a)(9)-5, A-1(d).

Distributions from a Roth IRA are not required during the account holder's lifetime. The RBD in the case of a Roth IRA is December 31 of the calendar year following the calendar year of the account holder's death. If the account holder's beneficiary is his or her surviving spouse, the spouse may roll the Roth IRA into his or her own Roth IRA or treat the deceased account holder's Roth IRA as his or her own Roth IRA. In other cases, the minimum distribution rules will apply after the account holder's death in the same manner as after the death of an account holder of a traditional IRA as if the participant died before his or her RBD.[126]

4. Distributions Upon Participant's Death Before RBD

If a participant dies before reaching his or her RBD and he or she has a designated beneficiary, the minimum distribution rules require that the deceased participant's plan benefits and IRAs be distributed over the designated beneficiary's life expectancy, beginning no later than the end of the calendar year after the calendar year of the participant's death.[127] If the participant's sole designated beneficiary is his or her surviving spouse, the distribution must commence by the end of the calendar year in which the participant would have reached age 70½, or, if later, December 31 of the calendar year following the calendar year of the participant's death (*i.e.*, the participant dies during the year in which he or she reaches or would have reached age 70½).[128]

If the plan benefit or IRA is payable to more than one beneficiary, and the surviving spouse is one of those beneficiaries, he or she will not be treated as the participant's sole beneficiary unless, by September 30 of the calendar year following the calendar year of the participant's death (the "beneficiary determination date"), the other beneficiary or beneficiaries have been cashed out, have disclaimed their right to receive the plan benefit or IRA, or a separate account has been created for the portion of the plan benefit or IRA to which the surviving spouse is entitled. The final regulations seem to allow the separate account to be established by the end of the calendar year following the calendar year of the participant's death.[129] However, if one of the beneficiaries as of the beneficiary designation date is not an individual, a separate account should be established for that beneficiary by the beneficiary determination date to

[126] § 408A(c)(5); Treas. Reg. § 1.408A-6, Q&A-14.
[127] Treas. Reg. § 1.401(a)(9)-3, A-3(a).
[128] Treas. Reg. § 1.401(a)(9)-3, A-3(b).
[129] Treas. Reg. § 1.401(a)(9)-8, A-2(a)(2).

ensure that the participant has a designated beneficiary. This is based on comments by Marjorie Hoffman, Senior Technician Reviewer, Tax Exempt/Government Entities, Internal Revenue Service, who is one of the authors of the final regulations, at an ALI-ABA Video Law Review Program on May 23, 2002 (referred to as "Marjorie Hoffman's comments").

Although the identity of the designated beneficiary is determined on the beneficiary determination date, the beneficiary must be someone who was named as the participant's beneficiary under the participant's beneficiary designation or under the plan as of the participant's date of death. Unless the surviving spouse is the participant's sole designated beneficiary, the life expectancy of the designated beneficiary is determined in the calendar year following the calendar year of the participant's death, and is reduced by one year for each year thereafter.[130] If the surviving spouse is the participant's sole designated beneficiary, while the spouse is alive the applicable distribution period is the spouse's life expectancy determined each year.[131] Once the spouse dies, the remaining applicable distribution period is the spouse's life expectancy in the calendar year of his or her death, reduced by one for each calendar year that has elapsed after the calendar year of the spouse's death.[132] The life expectancy of a designated beneficiary, including a spouse who is the participant's sole designated beneficiary, is determined under Reg. § 1.401(a)(9)-9, A-1. The life expectancy table is set out in Appendix B.[133] If the participant does not have a designated beneficiary by the beneficiary determination date, the participant's plan benefits or IRAs must be distributed by the end of the fifth calendar year following the calendar year of the participant's death[134]

Under the final regulations, the life expectancy rule applies unless there is no designated beneficiary or the plan provides that the five-year rule will apply. Depending upon the terms of the plan, a designated beneficiary may elect to have the five-year rule apply.[135] This may be advisable if the designated beneficiary's remaining life expectancy is less than five years. If the participant's sole designated beneficiary fails to take required minimum distributions in any of the first four calendar years following the

---

[130] Treas. Reg. § 1.401(a)(9)-5, A-5(c)(1).
[131] Treas. Reg. § 1.401(a)(9)-5, A-5(c)(2).
[132] Treas. Reg. § 1.401(a)(9)-5, A-5(c)(2).
[133] Treas. Reg. § 1.401(a)(9)-5, A-6.
[134] Code § 401(a)(9)(B)(ii).
[135] Treas. Reg. § 1.401(a)(9)-3, A-4(c).

calendar year of the participant's death, the regulations provide for an automatic waiver of the 50% excise tax if the designated beneficiary receives the entire remaining plan benefit or IRA by the end of the fifth calendar year following the calendar year of the participant's death.[136]

A plan may provide that the five-year rule always applies to certain types of distributions or applies to all distributions, and can apply different methods of distribution to different employees.[137]

5. *Distributions Upon Participant's Death After RBD*

If a participant dies after his or her RBD, and the participant has a designated beneficiary by the beneficiary determination date, the remaining plan benefit or IRA must be paid to the designated beneficiary over the longer of (a) the designated beneficiary's life expectancy, determined in the year following the calendar year of the participant's death; or (b) the participant's remaining life expectancy, determined in the year of the participant's death, in each case reduced by one year for each year thereafter, commencing by the end of the calendar year following the calendar year of the participant's death.[138] However, if the participant's sole designated beneficiary is the participant's spouse, the applicable distribution period is the spouse's life expectancy determined each year until his or her death, when it then becomes the life expectancy of the spouse determined in the calendar year of the surviving spouse's death, reduced by one for each calendar year that has elapsed after the calendar year of the spouse's death.[139] If there is no designated beneficiary by the beneficiary determination date, the applicable distribution period is the life expectancy of the participant determined in the year of his or her death, reduced by one year for each year thereafter.

6. *Spousal and Nonspousal Rollovers and Inherited IRAs*

Regardless of whether the participant dies before or after his or her RBD, if the spouse is the beneficiary of all or part of the participant's plan benefit or IRA, he or she may roll the plan benefit (if permitted under the plan) or IRA (or the part of which he or she is beneficiary) into his or her own IRA, or, in the case of an IRA, treat the decedent's IRA as his or her

[136] Treas. Reg. § 54.4974-2, A-7(b).
[137] Treas. Reg. § 1.401(a)(9)-3, A-4(b).
[138] Treas. Reg. § 1.401(a)(9)-5, A-5(a)(1) and (c)(1) and (3).
[139] Treas. Reg. § 1.401(a)(9)-5, A-5(a)(1) and (c)(2).

own IRA.[140] If the participant dies after his or her RBD, and the entire required minimum distribution for the year of the participant's death has not been distributed to him or her before his or her death, the balance of the required minimum distribution must be paid to the surviving spouse before the end of the year.[141] The election to treat the decedent's IRA as the spouse's IRA or to roll over the IRA to his or her own IRA may be made at any time after the participant's death.[142]

If the surviving spouse has already reached his or her RBD, he or she must begin receiving required minimum distributions under the uniform lifetime table in the year in which the rollover occurs, unless the rollover occurs in the year of the participant's death and the participant had already reached his or her RBD, in which case the spouse must take a required distribution for that year, determined with respect to the deceased participant, to the extent not distributed before the participant's death. The surviving spouse will not be able to elect to treat a deceased participant's IRA that is payable to a trust as his or her own IRA, but may still roll into his or her own IRA any distribution from the decedent's plan benefit or IRA to a trust to the extent that it is not a required minimum distribution if some or all of the distribution is redistributed to him or her.[143]

If the benefit is left in the deceased participant's plan or IRA (and the spouse does not elect to treat the IRA as his or her own IRA) and the surviving spouse dies before the distribution has begun, the five-year distribution rule and the exception to the five-year distribution rule apply as if the surviving spouse were the participant.[144] In determining whether distributions have commenced to the surviving spouse, payments, other than from irrevocable annuities, made before the date the payments are

[140] Code § 402(c)(9) and Treas. Reg. § 1.408-8, A-5(a).

[141] Treas. Reg. § 1.408-8, A-5(a).

[142] *Id.*

[143] Treas. Reg. § 1.408-8, A-5(a); preamble.

[144] Code § 401(a)(9)(B)(iv)(II); Treas. Reg. § 1.408-3, Q&A-5. S*ee also* Priv. Ltr. Rul. 200436017 (where amounts payable from decedent's qualified plan to surviving spouse were not distributed because of surviving spouse's death, and where such amounts remain in decedent's plan and the decedent did not designate a beneficiary, required minimum distributions with respect to such amounts will be subject to five-year rule of § 401(a)(9)(B)(ii)). However, the spousal exception to the five-year rule does not apply, so that if the surviving spouse remarries and names the new spouse as the designated beneficiary of the plan benefit or IRA and then dies, the new spouse will be treated as a nonspouse beneficiary. Of course, the new spouse may still do a spousal rollover.

required to begin are disregarded.[145] The spouse may designate a beneficiary to receive any remaining benefits. Payments to a minor child are treated as payments to the surviving spouse and will not disqualify the spouse from electing the spousal exception to the five-year distribution rule if payments of the benefit will be made only to the spouse after the child reaches majority.[146]

Effective for distributions after December 31, 2006, § 829 of the Pension Protection Act of 2006 permits qualified retirement plan benefits of a beneficiary other than a spouse to be transferred directly to an IRA, which is treated as an inherited IRA of the nonspouse beneficiary. To the extent provided by rules issued by the Treasury, benefits payable to a trust maintained for a designated beneficiary may also be transferred directly to an IRA, which will be treated as an inherited IRA. As a result of the new rule, a nonspouse beneficiary of a deceased participant in a qualified retirement plan should be able to have the benefit transferred directly to an IRA to allow the benefit to be paid over the maximum period permitted under the minimum distribution rules when the plan does not permit such an extended payout.

The IRS issued Notice 2007-7[147] to provide guidance dealing with the provisions of the Act affecting retirement arrangements, including the nonspousal rollover provisions. According to the guidance, a nonspousal rollover may be made to a trust if a beneficiary of the trust is treated as the designated beneficiary and the trust satisfies the four requirements specified in the regulations dealing with the minimum distribution rules. These require that the trust must be valid, the trust must be irrevocable at the participant's death, the beneficiaries entitled to the benefit must be identifiable, and certain documentation requirements must be satisfied. Although the guidance made it clear that a plan was not required to allow a nonspousal rollover, IRC §§ 401(a)(31) and 402(f)(2)(A) now require a plan to allow a nonspousal rollover. The guidance did not specify what action a plan must take to permit nonspousal rollovers. For example, does the plan have to be amended, or can the plan administrator simply allow nonspousal rollovers as an administrative matter?

---

[145] Treas. Reg. § 1.401(a)(9)-3, Q&A-6.

[146] Code § 401(a)(9)(F). The statute refers to regulations prescribed by the Treasury. Neither the 2001 proposed regulations nor the final regulations discuss this rule. The omission is important because if, without the rule, a child is entitled to receive benefits under the plan or IRA, the surviving spouse would not be treated as the sole beneficiary.

[147] 2007-5 I.R.B. 395.

The guidance also described how the minimum distribution rules apply to a nonspousal rollover. The ability to roll over some or all of a benefit and the applicable distribution period depend upon whether the decedent died before or after his or her required beginning date and when the nonspousal rollover occurs. If the decedent died before his or her RBD, the entire benefit may be rolled over in the year of the decedent's death, and the beneficiary must begin receiving distributions based on his or her life expectancy the following year. In any year after the decedent died, the beneficiary must take the required minimum distribution he or she would have received under the life expectancy method and may then roll the balance into an inherited IRA. Although the five-year rule applied to the plan benefit under the terms of the plan, the life expectancy method can be used if the rollover occurs in the year of the participant's death or the year following the year of the participant's death. If the beneficiary fails to take a minimum distribution in any of the first four years after the decedent died, he or she may still roll over the balance, but will now be required under the five-year rule to take the entire balance by the end of the fifth year after the decedent died.

If the decedent died after his or her RBD, any remaining minimum distribution the decedent would have been required to take in the year of death must be distributed before the balance can be rolled over. After the year of the decedent's death, the beneficiary must receive a distribution from the plan based on his or her life expectancy before rolling the balance into an inherited IRA. Thereafter, contributions may be made over his or her life expectancy, reduced by one year for each year thereafter.

7. Designated Beneficiary

A designated beneficiary must be an individual.[148] An individual beneficiary of a trust may be treated as a designated beneficiary if the trust meets the requirements discussed in this section.[149]

A participant's designated beneficiary after his or her death is determined as of the beneficiary determination date (September 30 of the year following the year of the participant's death).[150] However, if an individual who is a beneficiary as of the date of the participant's death dies before

---

[148] Treas. Reg. § 1.401(a)(9)-4, A-1.
[149] Treas. Reg. § 1.401(a)(9)-4, A-5.
[150] Treas. Reg. § 1.401(a)(9)-4, A-4(a).

the beneficiary determination date, the individual will continue to be treated as a beneficiary on the beneficiary determination date unless the individual has disclaimed the right to the benefit or IRA. Presumably, a deceased individual's personal representative may disclaim if so permitted under state law. It is not clear whether a beneficiary designation could require an individual to survive until the beneficiary determination date in order to be entitled to receive the benefit, and if the individual does not survive until then, the individual would not be taken into account in determining the designated beneficiary.

If there are two or more beneficiaries at the beneficiary determination date, only the oldest beneficiary will be treated as a designated beneficiary unless each beneficiary is entitled to a separate share or separate account.[151] If there are two or more beneficiaries at the beneficiary designation date and one of the beneficiaries is not an individual, the participant will be treated as not having any designated beneficiary unless the non-individual beneficiary is entitled to a separate share or a separate account.[152]

Separate accounts are separate portions of a participant's benefit reflecting the separate interests of the participant's beneficiaries under the plan as of the date of the participant's death for which separate accounting is maintained. The separate accounting must allocate all post-death investment gains and losses, contributions, and forfeitures for the period prior to the establishment of the separate accounts on a pro rata basis in a reasonable and consistent manner among the separate accounts. In addition, any post-death distribution to a beneficiary must reduce the separate account of that beneficiary. Once the separate accounts are actually established, the separate accounting can provide for separate investments for each separate account under which gains and losses from the investment of the account are only allocated to that account, or investment gains and losses can continue to be allocated among the separate accounts on a pro rata basis. The final regulations state that to be effective, the separate account must be established by the end of the calendar year following the calendar year of the participant's death.[153]

---

[151] Treas. Reg. § 1.401(a)(9)-5, A-7(a)(1).
[152] Treas. Reg. § 1.401(a)(9)-5, A-7(a)(2).
[153] Treas. Reg. § 1.401(a)(9)-8, A-2(a)(2).

Under the initial final regulations, if the separate accounts were not established until the end of the calendar year following the calendar year of the participant's death, the applicable distribution period for the first distribution year would have been based on the life expectancy of the oldest beneficiary of all the separate accounts. According to Marjorie Hoffman's comments, if the separate accounts were established by the beneficiary determination date, the applicable distribution period for each separate account for the first distribution year would have been based on the oldest beneficiary of that account. However, under the language of the initial final regulations, unless the separate accounts were established by the end of the calendar year in which the participant dies, the life expectancy of the oldest beneficiary of each separate account could not be used until the second distribution year (which would be the calendar year following the calendar year following the calendar year of the participant's death). The final regulations were amended in 2004 to provide that the applicable distribution period would be the age of the oldest beneficiary of each separate account if the separate accounts were established by the end of the calendar year following the participant's death.[154] Also according to Marjorie Hoffman's comments, as mentioned earlier, if a separate account is to be established for a beneficiary who is not an individual, it is advisable to establish the separate account for that beneficiary by the beneficiary determination date to ensure that the participant has a designated beneficiary. It is not clear what is meant by "establishing" a separate account. Because "establishing" a separate account may require that the plan sponsor or IRA administrator create separate accounts with separate reporting, designating beneficiaries as entitled to fractional shares of an account may not be sufficient to establish separate accounts.

An individual, to be treated as a designated beneficiary, must be designated under the terms of the plan, including an affirmative election by the participant pursuant to the terms of the plan.[155] An individual who becomes entitled to the benefit under applicable state law is not a designated beneficiary.[156] The final regulations provide that a participant will not have a designated beneficiary if his or her estate is the named beneficiary, even though an individual becomes entitled to receive the benefit by the beneficiary determination date.[157] The preamble to the final

[154] Treasury Decision 9130.
[155] Treas. Reg. § 1.401(a)(9)-4, A-1.
[156] *Id.*
[157] Treas. Reg. § 1.401(a)(9)-4, A-1.

regulations clarifies that a trust will not fail to be treated as a trust merely because the trust elects to be treated as an estate under § 645, as long as the trust continues to be a trust under state law.

There are three ways that the identity of the designated beneficiary can be changed after the participant's death but before the beneficiary determination date. First, one or more beneficiaries may be cashed out, *i.e.*, they receive the entire amount of the plan benefit or IRA to which they are entitled.[158] For example, if a participant has named a charitable organization as the beneficiary of the first $100,000 of his plan benefit or IRA and an individual as the beneficiary of the remaining portion, the participant would not be treated as having a designated beneficiary after his or her death under the 1987 proposed regulations because the charity's right would not be treated as a separate account. However, under the final regulations, if $100,000 is paid to the charity before the beneficiary determination date, the charity will no longer be considered in determining whether the participant has a designated beneficiary. Second, one or more beneficiaries may disclaim their right to receive the plan benefit or IRA, pursuant to a qualified disclaimer under § 2518.[159]

Third, separate accounts may be established for each beneficiary before the beneficiary determination date.[160] For example, if the benefits are payable in equal shares to the participant's three children and to a grandchild (the child of a predeceased child), and separate accounts are established before the end of the calendar year following the calendar year of the participant's death, each child and the grandchild may take distributions from his or her separate account based on his or her life expectancy, rather than the life expectancy of the oldest child.

The final regulations provide that if a beneficiary's entitlement to a participant's benefit or IRA is contingent on an event other than the participant's death or the death of another beneficiary, the contingent beneficiary is considered in determining which designated beneficiary has the shortest life expectancy and whether any beneficiary is not an individual.[161] A person will not be considered a beneficiary for purposes of determining who is the beneficiary with the shortest life expectancy or whether a person who is not an individual is a beneficiary merely because

---

[158] Treas. Reg. § 1.401(a)(9)-4, A-4(a).
[159] Treas. Reg. § 1.401(a)(9)-4, A-4(a).
[160] *See* Treas. Reg. § 1.401(a)(9)-8, A-2(a)(2).
[161] Treas. Reg. § 1.401(a)(9)-5, A-7(b).

the person could become the successor to the interest of one of the beneficiaries after the beneficiary's death. This exception does not apply to a person who has any right (including a contingent right) to a participant's benefit beyond a mere potential successor to the interest of one of the beneficiaries upon that beneficiary's death.[162] For example, if the first beneficiary has a right to all income with respect to a participant's individual account during the beneficiary's life and a second beneficiary has a right to the principal but only after the death of the first income beneficiary (any portion of the principal distributed during the life of the first income beneficiary to be held in trust until that first beneficiary's death), both beneficiaries must be taken into account in determining the beneficiary with the shortest life expectancy and whether only individuals are beneficiaries.

Although the Treasury apparently has not reached a definitive position on the subject, Marjorie Hoffman's comments expressed her opinion that if income was payable to a beneficiary with the remainder to the beneficiary's child at the beneficiary's death, and, if the child does not survive the beneficiary, to a charitable organization, the charitable organization would not be treated as a beneficiary in determining whether there was a beneficiary as of the beneficiary determination date who was not an individual. Marjorie Hoffman also indicated approval of the position in Priv. Ltr. Rul. 200228025, which held that where a benefit was payable to a trust for the benefit of two children, and if both those children died before reaching age 30, the benefit was payable to the participant's brother, who was age 67, the life expectancy of the brother had to be used for determining the applicable distribution period, even though each child was to have received the child's share of the benefit if the child survived until age 30, and if one child died before age 30, that child's share was added to the share of the other child.

If the designated beneficiary whose life expectancy is being used to calculate the distribution period dies after the beneficiary determination date, such beneficiary's remaining life expectancy will be used to determine the distribution period, whether or not a beneficiary with a shorter life expectancy becomes entitled to receive the plan benefit or IRA.[163]

---

[162] Treas. Reg. § 1.401(a)(9)-5, A-7(c)(1).
[163] Treas. Reg. § 1.401(a)(9)-5, A-7(c)(2).

8. *Trustee as Beneficiary*

The final regulations did not change the requirements that a trust must satisfy in order to have the oldest individual beneficiary of the trust treated as a participant's designated beneficiary. However, the time by which these requirements must be satisfied has been affected by the use of the uniform lifetime table. In addition, the regulations clarify when a spouse will be treated as the sole beneficiary of a trust. In order for an individual who is the beneficiary of a trust to be treated as the participant's designated beneficiary, the trust must satisfy the following four requirements during any period during which required minimum distributions are being determined by taking into account the designated beneficiary's life expectancy: (1) the trust must be a valid trust or would be a valid trust under state law if it had a corpus; (2) the beneficiaries of the trust entitled to the plan benefit or IRA must be identifiable; (3) the trust must be either irrevocable or, by its terms, will become irrevocable at the participant's death; and (4) certain documentation requirements must be satisfied.[164]

Unless the participant's sole designated beneficiary is his or her spouse and the spouse is more than ten years younger than the participant, the first three requirements must be satisfied by the beneficiary determination date, and the documentation requirements must be satisfied by October 31 of the year following the year of the participant's death.[165] In this case, because the uniform lifetime table is used for determining the required minimum distribution while the participant is alive, the life expectancy of a designated beneficiary is irrelevant.

If the spouse is the participant's sole designated beneficiary and is more than ten years younger than the participant, however, these requirements must be satisfied at the beginning of the calendar year in which the spouse becomes the sole designated beneficiary if the participant wishes to use the joint and last survivor expectancy of the husband and wife rather than the uniform lifetime table for determining the required minimum distribution for that year. In this case, the spouse's life expectancy is relevant in determining the joint and last survivor expectancy of the participant and his or her spouse each year.

---

[164] Treas. Reg. § 1.401(a)(9)-4, A-5.

[165] Treas. Reg. § 1.401(a)(9)-4, A-6(b).

The requirement that the trust beneficiaries entitled to the plan benefits or IRAs be identifiable is necessary because the age of the oldest beneficiary is required to calculate the minimum distribution after the participant's death (or after the RBD if the participant's sole beneficiary is his or her spouse and the spouse is more than ten years younger than the participant). If there are any beneficiaries of the trust entitled to the plan benefits or IRAs that do not qualify as designated beneficiaries for purposes of calculating minimum distributions, such as charities or creditors (*e.g.,* funeral expenses), the participant may be treated as not having a designated beneficiary.[166]

Because the payment of a benefit to a trust qualifies as a distribution for purposes of the minimum distribution rules, the trust is not required to redistribute the payment to a beneficiary.[167] Consequently, the trustee may accumulate plan and IRA distributions in the trust until the beneficiary has a particular need or reaches a designated age. But note that if all distributions to the trust are not required to be paid out to the surviving spouse, the spouse will not be treated as the sole beneficiary.[168]

Unfortunately, the final regulations require that separate accounts be established in the beneficiary designation form, and simply naming a trust that has separate shares for different beneficiaries will not create separate accounts for purposes of the minimum distribution rules.[169] However, Priv. Ltr. Rul. 2002234074, although decided under the 1987 proposed regulations, indicated that separate accounts may be established for minimum distribution purposes when the trust is to be immediately divided into separate trusts after the participant's death.

Priv. Ltr. Rul. 200537044 confirms that naming, in a beneficiary designation form, separate trusts created under an existing trust at the death of the participant will establish separate accounts for each separate trust, so that the oldest individual beneficiary of each trust will be treated as the designated beneficiary with respect to the share of the IRA payable to the separate trust. Note: In this ruling, the designation form named the separate trusts and not the preexisting trust as the beneficiary of the IRA.

---

[166] Priv. Ltr. Rul. 9820021.

[167] Treas. Reg. § 1.401(a)(9)-8, Q&A-11.

[168] Treas. Reg. § 1.401(a)(9)-5, Q&A-7, *Examples 1 and 2*; 2001 Prop. Treas. Reg. § 1.401(a)(9)-5, Q&A-7, *Examples 2 and 3*.

[169] Treas. Reg. § 1.401(a)(9)-4, A-5(c), adopting the position in Priv. Ltr. Rul. 199903050.

To satisfy the documentation requirements, the participant or trustee must furnish to the plan administrator, by October 31 of the calendar year following the calendar year of the participant's death, either the trust instrument or a list of beneficiaries, including contingent and remainder beneficiaries, and the conditions on their entitlement. In addition, the participant or trustee must certify that the list is complete and agree to furnish a copy of the trust instrument if requested by the plan administrator and that the other three requirements described earlier are satisfied. If the spouse is the sole designated beneficiary and is more than ten years younger than the participant, these requirements apply at the beginning of the year in which such a spouse becomes the participant's sole designated beneficiary or, apparently, the RBD in the case of the first required minimum distribution, if the participant wants to use the joint and last survivor expectancy of the participant and the spouse redetermined each year in lieu of the uniform lifetime table for that year. In this case, if the trust agreement is amended during the participant's lifetime, a copy of the amendment or corrected certification, if the amendment changes the information certified, must be furnished to the plan administrator within a reasonable time.[170]

The documentation requirements are overbroad, as in many cases there will be numerous contingent and remainder beneficiaries that will have to be listed, as well as a description of how they will become entitled to receive a benefit. Only the name and age of the oldest beneficiary of each separate share of the trust that is a beneficiary of the trust with respect to a plan benefit or IRA is needed by the plan administrator to determine the required minimum distribution. A plan administrator will not usually be qualified to interpret the terms of a trust agreement.

No documentation should be required to be provided to the financial institution sponsoring an IRA, because IRA sponsors are not responsible for determining required minimum distributions and the account holder may take the total of the required minimum distributions calculated separately for each of his or her IRAs from any one or more of his or her IRAs.[171] For example, assume that a participant has four IRAs and that each IRA has an account balance as of the end of the previous calendar year of $500,000, for a total amount in all four IRAs of $2,000,000. Assume also that the applicable distribution period is 10 years, so the

---

[170] Treas. Reg. § 1.401(a)(9)-4, A-6.
[171] Treas. Reg. § 1.408-8, A-9.

required minimum distribution will be $200,000 (10% of $2,000,000). The participant could take the aggregate required minimum distribution of $200,000 (10% of $2,000,000) from one IRA, $50,000 from each IRA, or any variation thereof. Consequently, each IRA sponsor may never know whether the account holder was taking his or her required minimum distribution in any given year. Inherited IRAs may not be aggregated with IRAs in the individual's own name, but IRAs inherited from the same decedent may be aggregated for purposes of determining the required minimum distributions from all of such IRAs and the required minimum distribution may be taken from any of such inherited IRAs.[172]

However, the final regulations now require the trustee, custodian, or issuer of an IRA to report certain information in a manner to be prescribed by revenue rulings, notices, and other guidance.[173] At the same time as the final regulations were issued, the IRS issued Notice 2002-27, dealing with the reporting requirements for trustees, custodians, and issuers of IRAs. Effective beginning with required distributions for 2003, an IRA owner must be provided, by January 31 of the calendar year in which a required minimum distribution is required, either a statement of the amount of the required minimum distribution or a statement that a minimum distribution is required for the year and the date by which the amount must be distributed, and an offer to furnish the IRA owner, upon request, the amount of the required minimum distribution. Notice 2003-3, I.R.B. 2002-18, 814, permits trustees to satisfy the first alternative for some of its customers and the second alternative for other customers and to transmit the statements electronically. Beginning with required minimum distributions for calendar year 2004, the trustee of an IRA must notify the IRS on Form 5498 that a minimum distribution is required with respect to an IRA for the calendar year, but need not indicate the amount, and must inform the IRA owner that it will be reporting such information to the IRS. Currently, no reporting is required for participants in 403(b) deferred annuity plans or beneficiaries of IRA owners.

If a trust is the beneficiary of a qualified plan benefit or IRA, the question arises as to which beneficiaries of the trust must be considered in determining who is the oldest beneficiary and whether any beneficiary is not an individual. If at least one beneficiary of the trust that must be considered for this purpose is not an individual, such as a charitable

[172] Treas. Reg. § 408-8, A-9.

[173] Treas. Reg. § 1.408-8, A-10.

organization, then the participant will be treated as not having a designated beneficiary. Apparently, any potential beneficiary of the trust, including a non-individual beneficiary or a beneficiary who is older than the apparent designated beneficiary, must be taken into account in determining whether there is a "designated beneficiary" under the minimum distribution rules, unless such beneficiary would only become entitled to receive distributions from the plan or IRA if one or more prior individual beneficiaries have died prematurely. Consequently, a beneficiary of a trust can be disregarded as a beneficiary if he or she or it will become entitled to receive some of the plan benefit or IRA only if either he, she, or it survives another beneficiary who would receive the balance of the plan benefit or IRA if he or she were alive at the relevant event (such as the death of the individual who was the original designated beneficiary). In addition, if all distributions from the plan or IRA made to the trust must be redistributed to the beneficiary who is desired to be treated as the designated beneficiary while he or she is alive, other trust beneficiaries will be disregarded in determining the identity of the designated beneficiary. Such a trust is referred to as a *conduit trust*.

For example, if a participant names a trust as his or her beneficiary, and under the terms of the trust the oldest beneficiary is the participant's spouse, and following the spouse's death the assets of the trust, including the right to receive the remaining plan benefit or IRA, are payable in equal shares to the participant's children who survive the spouse, and if there are no children then living, to a charitable organization, the charitable organization would not be considered in determining whether the participant had a designated beneficiary, because its entitlement to receive some of the plan benefit or IRA depends on none of the participant's children surviving the spouse. On the other hand, if the trust agreement provided that the trust continued in existence after the spouse's death for the benefit of the then living children, and at the death of the last child to die the assets were payable to the charitable organization, the charitable organization would be considered in determining whether the participant had a designated beneficiary unless all distributions from the plan or IRA were required to be distributed to the spouse when received by the trust. While this interpretation appears to be consistent with the example in the regulations discussed later in this section, some commentators believe that, until there is further guidance from the IRS, the trust agreement should provide that in no event will the plan benefit or IRA be paid to an individual older than the intended designated beneficiary or to a beneficiary who is not an individual. This could be accomplished, for example, by providing if at any time there is only one surviving individual beneficiary of a trust while a plan benefit or IRA is still payable to the trust, the right to receive the plan benefit or IRA would be assigned to that individual beneficiary.[174]

In addition, the terms of the trust should not direct that, after the beneficiary determination date, plan benefits or IRAs distributed to the trust be used to pay debts or expenses of the participant's estate, including federal and state estate and death taxes; otherwise, the participant may not be treated as having a designated beneficiary because the participant's estate could be treated as a beneficiary of the plan benefit or IRA. No one should have a general power of appointment with respect to the plan benefit or IRA, including any amount distributed to the trust, and special powers of appointment should be limited to individuals who are younger than the individual whom the participant wants to be the designated beneficiary. However, the individual whom the participant wants to be the designated beneficiary may have an unlimited right of withdrawal.

None of these rules that have apparently been imposed by the IRS in private letter rulings makes any policy sense, since in every case the distributions to the trust will have been subject to income tax and more than likely at a higher rate than if paid to an individual beneficiary because it will have been taxable to a trust, which is usually in a higher federal income tax bracket than an individual. In addition, if an individual had been named as the sole outright beneficiary instead of a trust, the balance of the plan benefit or IRA held by the individual, plus any remaining plan benefit or IRA not yet distributed, could be payable to either an older beneficiary or a non-individual beneficiary without affecting the status of the individual as the designated beneficiary (but in this case, the individual beneficiary would have received all distributions while alive). Note that some of these unfavorable consequences can be eliminated before the beneficiary determination date by cashing out certain beneficiaries, by having certain beneficiaries disclaim their interests, and by segregating plan benefits or account balances into separate accounts.

The final regulations provide two examples that confirm the IRS's position taken in Rev. Rul. 2000-2, I.R.B. 2000-3, relating to the qualification for the marital deduction of a plan benefit or IRA payable to a qualified terminable interest property (QTIP) trust, and clarify when a

---

[174] *See* Treas. Reg. § 1.401(a)(9)-5, A-7(b) and (c)(3), *Examples 1 and 2*.

surviving spouse will be treated as the participant's sole designated beneficiary when the spouse is a beneficiary of a trust to which the plan benefit or IRA is payable.

In the first example, the participant dies in 2001 at the age of 55, survived by the participant's spouse, who is 50 years old. The participant has named the trustee of a testamentary trust established under the participant's will as the beneficiary of all amounts payable from the participant's account in a defined contribution plan. It is stated that the participant's account balance is invested only in productive assets. Further, by October 31 of the calendar year following the calendar year of the participant's death, a copy of the trust agreement and a list of the trust beneficiaries are provided to the plan administrator. At the participant's death, the trust was irrevocable and was a valid trust under the laws of the state of the participant's domicile. The participant's account balance was includable in the participant's gross estate under § 2039. Under the terms of the trust, all trust income is payable annually to the spouse, and no one has the power to appoint the trust principal to any person other than the spouse. The participant's children, who are all younger than the spouse, are the sole remainder beneficiaries of the trust. No other person has a beneficial interest in the trust. Under the terms of the trust, the spouse has the power, exercisable annually, to compel the trustee to withdraw from the participant's account balance an amount equal to the income earned on the assets in the account during the calendar year and to distribute that amount through the trust to the spouse. The plan contains no prohibition on withdrawals from the participant's account of amounts in excess of the annual required minimum distributions.

In accordance with the terms of the plan, the trustee of the trust elects to receive annual required minimum distributions using the life expectancy rule for distributions over a distribution period equal to the spouse's life expectancy. If the spouse exercises the withdrawal power, the trustee must withdraw from the participant's account the greater of the amount of income earned in the account during the calendar year or the required minimum distribution. However, under the terms of the trust, as well as applicable state law, only the portion of the plan distribution received by the trustee equal to the income earned by the assets in the account is required to be distributed to the spouse, along with any other trust income. Because some amounts distributed from the plan to the trust may be accumulated in the trust during the spouse's lifetime for the benefit of the children, as remainder beneficiaries of the trust, even though access to those amounts is delayed until after the spouse's death, the children are treated as beneficiaries of the participant's plan benefit in addition to the spouse, and the spouse therefore is not the sole beneficiary. Although the spouse's life expectancy, determined in the calendar year following the participant's death, will be used for purposes of determining the required minimum distributions to the trust, the spouse's life expectancy will not be redetermined each year as it would have been had the spouse been the participant's sole designated beneficiary. Instead, the spouse's life expectancy will be reduced by one for each year that elapses. In addition, the distributions to the spouse must commence by the end of the calendar year following the calendar year of the participant's death, rather than by the end of the year in which the participant would have reached age 70½.[175]

In the second example, the facts are the same, except that the trust requires that the trustee pay all amounts distributed from the plan to the trustee while the spouse is alive directly to the spouse upon receipt. In this case, the spouse is the sole beneficiary of the participant's plan benefit for purposes of determining the designated beneficiary, because no amounts distributed from the plan to the trust are accumulated in the trust during the spouse's lifetime for the benefit of any other beneficiary. Consequently, the annual required minimum distributions may be postponed until the end of the calendar year in which the participant would have reached age 70½. Although the example does not so state, because the spouse is the sole designated beneficiary, the spouse's life expectancy may be redetermined each year for purposes of determining the required minimum distribution to the trust while the spouse is alive.[176]

9. Effective Dates

The final regulations are effective for determining required minimum distributions after 2002. Beneficiaries must use the final regulations after 2002 even though the participant died before 2003.[177] In the case of a participant who died before 2003, the designated beneficiary must be determined under the final regulations for determining required minimum distributions for distributions after 2002. This may require that the designated beneficiary and the applicable distribution period be determined

---

[175] Treas. Reg. § 1.401(a)(9)-5, A-7(c)(3), *Example 1.*
[176] Treas. Reg. § 1.401(a)(9)-5, A-7(c)(3), *Example 2.*
[177] Treas. Reg. § 1.401(a)(9)-1, A-2(b)(1).

based on the final regulations applied at the time the identity of the designated beneficiary would have been initially determined under the new rules. Under the 1987 proposed regulations, the designated beneficiary would have been determined at the earlier of a participant's death or the participant's RBD. Under the 2001 proposed regulations, the designated beneficiary would have been determined as of December 31 of the calendar year following the calendar year of the participant's death. In addition, under the 2001 proposed regulations, if a beneficiary named as of the participant's death died before the beneficiary determination date, such beneficiary was not taken into account for purposes of determining the identity of the designated beneficiary.

10. Conclusion

The final regulations are certainly a vast improvement over the 1987 proposed regulations and eliminated some of the problems under the 2001 proposed regulations. However, a number of issues remain. It is unfortunate that an individual beneficiary of an estate or an individual who takes under a state's anti-lapse statute cannot be a designated beneficiary. It would have been preferable if the regulations would have provided that separate accounts with respect to individual beneficiaries of separate trusts could be created in the trust agreement itself, in addition to the beneficiary designation form. This would have allowed the participant to simply name a trust as beneficiary, and the trust terms could have created the separate shares.

The final regulations do not contain the provision contained in the 2001 proposed regulations that permitted either the participant or the participant's beneficiary who was treated as a designated beneficiary to designate a subsequent beneficiary for distributions of any portion of the participant's benefit or IRA remaining after the designated beneficiary died. Hopefully, this does not mean that a participant or the participant's beneficiary may not have such a right without jeopardizing beneficiary's status as a designated beneficiary.

It is unfortunate that the final regulations provide that a beneficiary named as of the participant's death who dies before the beneficiary determination date must still be taken into account in determining the oldest beneficiary. For example, if the participant named his or her spouse as his or her primary beneficiary and a child younger than the spouse as the contingent beneficiary, and the spouse survives the participant but dies before the beneficiary determination date, the spouse's shorter life expectancy will be the applicable distribution period rather than the participant's child's life expectancy. It is hoped that a deceased beneficiary's personal representative could disclaim his or her interest in the plan benefit or IRA if the beneficiary dies within nine months of the participant's death.

The position taken by the regulations was in response to concerns by commentators that if all the beneficiaries named by the participant or the plan as of the participant's death die before the beneficiary determination date, the participant would not have a designated beneficiary. Of course, careful planning would have provided for successor beneficiaries to take into account the death of an individual named as a beneficiary before the beneficiary determination date. The problem could have been solved by providing that a beneficiary who died before the beneficiary determination date would only be taken into account for purposes of determining whether the participant had a designated beneficiary if that was the only way to avoid the participant being treated as not having a designated beneficiary.

A participant should be able to condition a beneficiary's right to receive a plan benefit or IRA on surviving until the beneficiary determination date, and, if the beneficiary dies before then, he or she will not be considered a beneficiary. This could jeopardize the marital deduction in the case of a spouse who is named as the beneficiary. However, the spouse's right could be conditioned on surviving the participant for six months without disqualifying the plan benefit or IRA for the marital deduction. It is imperative that the spouse name a designated beneficiary as soon as possible after the participant dies if the participant dies before the RBD, or do a spousal rollover to ensure that when the spouse dies, there will be a designated beneficiary. Note that for purposes of naming a beneficiary, if the surviving spouse is the sole beneficiary, the spouse is treated as the participant until the participant would have reached age 70½, so that he or she can name a beneficiary that will be treated as a designated beneficiary for purposes of the minimum distribution rules if he or she dies before the deceased participant would have reached age 70½.

The final regulations should have clarified what beneficiaries of a trust must be taken into account for purposes of determining the oldest beneficiary and whether there are any beneficiaries who are not individuals. In addition, the final regulations should have clarified what "establishing" a separate account means and whether a separate account established by the beneficiary determination date would be effective for determining the required minimum distribution for the first distribution calendar year.

D. Excess Retirement Distributions and Accumulations

In TRA 86, Congress imposed a 15 percent excise tax on excess retirement distributions and excess retirement accumulations, to discourage excessive deferrals through the use of qualified retirement plans and IRAs.[178] The tax on excess retirement distributions was imposed on distributions from qualified retirement plans and IRAs received during a calendar year in excess of the greater of $150,000 or the indexed amount, referred to as the *annual threshold amount.*[179] The indexed amount, which began as $112,500, was $160,000 for 1997.[180] The tax on excess retirement accumulations was imposed on the excess of the value of a decedent's qualified retirement plan benefits and IRAs over the greater of a hypothetical annuity or a grandfathered amount. TRA 97 repealed the 15 percent excise tax, effective for distributions and decedents dying after 1996.

---

178 Code §§ 4980A(a), 4980A(d)(1); Temp. Reg. § 54.4981A-1T. (TAMRA § 1011A(g)(1)(A) redesignated Code § 4981A to § 4980A, but the temporary regulations were issued using the original Code section numbers.)
179 Code § 4980A(c)(I); Temp. Reg. § 54.4981A-IT, Q&A a-2.
180 IRS News Release IR-91-12 (Jan. 17, 1991).

Chapter Three

Income Taxation of Benefits

A. In General

Distributions from qualified retirement plans and traditional IRAs generally are taxed as ordinary income in the same manner as payments received under an annuity.[181] Qualified distributions from Roth IRAs are not taxed.[182] Nonqualified distributions from Roth IRAs are taxed to the extent that amounts distributed exceed contributions made that have not previously been distributed, which would be income earned on such contributions after the conversion to the Roth IRA.[183] Because the constructive receipt doctrine does not apply to any undistributed benefits from qualified retirement plans or IRAs, the distributions are taxed when actually received, even if the participant has the unrestricted right to withdraw the benefits at any time.[184]

Withholding of income tax on distributions from qualified retirement plans and IRAs is required unless the recipient elects not to have the tax withheld.[185] The payor is required to provide notice to the recipient concerning his or her right to elect not to have taxes withheld.[186] The election may be revoked by the recipient at any time before a distribution is made.[187] However, as discussed in Section H of this chapter, an eligible rollover distribution is subject to a mandatory 20 percent withholding, unless the distribution is directly transferred to an IRA or another qualified retirement plan.[188]

B. Taxable Portion of Qualified Retirement Plan and Traditional IRA Distributions

A participant or his or her beneficiary who receives a distribution from a qualified retirement plan or a traditional IRA is entitled to exclude from

[181] Code §§ 402(a)(1), 408(d)(1).
[182] Code § 408A(d)(1).
[183] Code § 408A(d)(1).
[184] Code §§ 402(a), 408(d)(1).
[185] Code §§ 3405(a)(2), (b)(2).
[186] Treas. Reg. § 35.3405-1T, Q&A d-3.
[187] Treas. Reg. § 35.3405-1, Q&A-12.
[188] Code § 3405(c).

income the participant's basis in the plan or IRA (also referred to as the participant's investment in the contract). The participant or beneficiary recovers the participant's basis ratably over the expected period of the distribution (*e.g.,* the participant's life expectancy).[189]

If the annuity starting date (generally the date regular payments of the participant's benefit begin under the plan) occurred on or before July 1, 1986, once the exclusion amount has been determined, the same amount continues to be excluded each year regardless of whether the aggregate amount eventually exceeds the participant's basis in the plan.[190] If the annuity starting date occurs after July 1, 1986, the total amount excluded may not exceed the participant's basis in the plan. Once the basis in the plan is recovered because the participant outlives his or her life expectancy, the entire amount received each year is taxable.[191]

The balance of the participant's basis in the plan remaining at the death of the last person entitled to any of the participant's benefit under the plan is deductible on that person's final income tax return.[192] The deduction is not limited by the 2 percent floor on miscellaneous itemized deductions.[193]

For example, assume that the participant is to receive an annuity of $20,000 a year payable for the participant's lifetime only, that the participant's life expectancy is 15 years, and that the participant has made nondeductible contributions of $30,000 (the participant's basis in the plan). The $30,000 will be recovered at the rate of $2,000 each year during the 15-year period, reducing the taxable amount of the annual distribution to $18,000. After the 15th year, the entire annual payment of $20,000 will be taxable each year. If the participant dies before receiving 15 payments, the balance of the participant's basis can be deducted from the participant's gross income on his or her final return.

A participant's basis in the plan includes nondeductible participant contributions,[194] amounts includible in the income of the participant

---

[189] Code § 72(b)(1).
[190] Code § 72(b), before the amendment by TRA 86.
[191] Code § 72(b)(2).
[192] Code § 72(b)(3)(A).
[193] Code § 72(b)(3)(C). *See* Internal Revenue Service Publication 575, *Pension and Annuity Income.*
[194] These are considered premiums paid by the participant.

attributable to life insurance coverage,[195] and the repayment of any loan that was treated as a taxable distribution because the loan exceeded the limit or failed to satisfy the requirements under Code § 72(p).[196] Any amounts distributed to the participant before the annuity starting date that were treated as a return of the participant's basis will reduce the amount of the participant's basis in the plan.

Before the Small Business Act, the IRS had provided a simplified method for calculating the amount of each payment that was treated as a tax-free return of the participant's basis in the plan.[197] Referred to as the *simplified general rule*, this method was available only if the annuity starting date was after July 1, 1986; the annuity payments were for either the life of the participant or the joint lives and life of the survivor of the participant and the participant's beneficiary; the annuity payments were from a qualified retirement plan; and as of the annuity starting date, the participant was either under age 75 or, if 75 or older, the number of years of guaranteed payments was fewer than five.

Under the simplified general rule, the amount of each payment treated as a tax-free return of the participant's basis in the plan was determined by dividing the participant's basis in the plan by a number determined by the participant's age under the following table and multiplying the result by the number of monthly payments received during the taxable year.

Age of Participant	*Number of Payments*
55 and under	300
56–60	260
61–65	240
66–70	170
71 and over	120

For example, assume that a participant reached age 61 in 1991, retired, and began to receive his or her benefits on September 1 of that year. Assume also that the participant had a basis in the plan equal to $24,000. The amount deemed to be recovered each month would be $100, determined by dividing $24,000 by 240. Since the participant would receive four

[195] Treas. Reg. § 1.72-16(b)(4).

[196] Code § 72(e)(4). Note that § 1402(a) of the Small Business Act repealed the $5,000 exclusion of employee death benefits from federal AGI that was formerly contained in Code § 101(b).

[197] IRS News Release IR-89-31 (Mar. 20, 1989).

payments in 1991, the participant would be able to exclude $400 from his or her annuity payments received during 1991 for income tax purposes.

The Small Business Act adopted a modified version of the simplified general rule as the only method for determining the amount of an annuity payment that is excludible from income because of the recipient's basis in the annuity. The amount of the distribution that is excluded from each monthly payment is determined under the following table:[198]

If the Age of the Primary Annuitant on the Annuity Starting Date Is:	*The Number of Anticipated Payments Is:*
Not more than 55	360
More than 55 but not more than 60	310
More than 60 but not more than 65	260
More than 65 but not more than 70	210
More than 70	160

TRA 97 added the following table that must be used for the simplified method when there are two or more annuitants:[199]

Combined Ages of Annuitants	*The Number of Anticipated Payments Is:*
Not more than 110	410
More than 110 but not more than 120	360
More than 120 but not more than 130	310
More than 130 but not more than 140	260
More than 140	210

In any case where the annuity payments are not made on a monthly basis, appropriate adjustments in the application of the table will be made to take into account the period on the basis of which the payments are made. The new simplified method does not apply where the primary annuitant has attained age 75 on the annuity starting date unless there are fewer than five years of guaranteed payments under the annuity.[200] If the tables cannot be used, the normal rules for taxing an annuity will apply; *i.e.,* the amount excluded from income is determined based on the annuitant's life expectancy.

---

[198] The Small Business Act § 1403.
[199] TRA 97 § 1075, amending Code § 72(d)(1)(B).
[200] Code § 72(d)(1)(E), as amended by the Small Business Act § 1403(a).

If the annuitant receives a lump sum, the lump sum will be taxable as if received before the annuity starting date, in which case it will be treated as taxable to the extent the value of the annuity exceeds the participant's basis in the annuity.[201] The annuity will then be taxed using the required method for annuities after subtracting the value of the lump sum and the basis recovered against the lump sum.

The three-year recovery rule that existed before July 1, 1986, for certain distributions was repealed by TRA 86 for annuities beginning after July 1, 1986.[202] Under the three-year recovery rule, if an individual could recover the participant's basis in the plan over the first three years of annuity payments, then none of the payments were subject to income until all the basis in the plan had been received.

If the participant withdraws amounts from the plan before the annuity starting date, the amount treated as a return of nondeductible employee contributions generally is determined by multiplying the amount of the current distribution by a fraction. The numerator of the fraction is the total amount of nondeductible employee contributions less nondeductible employee contributions previously treated as distributed. The denominator of the fraction is the total amount of the participant's account at the time of the distribution.[203]

In the case of either a defined contribution plan or a defined benefit plan that establishes a separate account for employee contributions and earnings on such contributions, the denominator is changed to the total nondeductible employee contributions and earnings on such contributions, and does not include the portion of the plan account attributable to employer contributions.[204] Therefore, the taxable amount will be limited to the earnings on the amount withdrawn and will not include employer contributions or earnings on those contributions.

A transition rule permits an employee to withdraw employee contributions made before January 1, 1987, to a plan that, as of May 5, 1986, permitted distributions of employee contributions before separation from service, without any part of the distribution being treated as earnings.[205]

[201] Code §§ 72(d)(1)(D), (e)(3), as amended by the Small Business Act § 1403(a).
[202] TRA 86 § 1122(c)(1) repealed former Code § 72(d).
[203] Code §§ 72(e)(2)(B), (8)(B).
[204] Code § 72(d).
[205] Code § 72(e)(8)(D).

Consequently, distributions of grandfathered nondeductible employee contributions will be completely nontaxable. The transition rule will continue to apply to grandfathered benefits transferred to another plan (by merger or plan-to-plan transfer) even if the transferred plan did not permit in-service distributions.[206]

For example, assume that a participant made $10,000 of nondeductible contributions to a plan after 1986, and in 1997, when the total of nondeductible employee contributions and earnings on those contributions was $20,000, wished to withdraw $5,000 from the plan. Since the fraction is one-half ($10,000 over $20,000), the participant must include $2,500 in gross income. The $2,500 may also be subject to the 10 percent penalty on premature distributions if the participant is under age 59½. If at least $5,000 of the participant's contributions had been made before 1987, and the plan permitted in-service withdrawals of nondeductible employee contributions as of May 5, 1986, none of the withdrawn amount would be taxable.

A distribution to an alternate payee who is a spouse or former spouse pursuant to a QDRO is taxed to the alternate payee in the same manner as it would be to the participant, and the participant's basis in the plan is allocated ratably between the participant and the alternate payee.[207] If the alternate payee is not the spouse or a former spouse of the participant, the participant will be taxed on the distributions.[208] For example, distributions made to a participant's children pursuant to a QDRO are includible in the participant's income and not the children's income. However, if the participant does not elect out of withholding, the amount actually received by the child will be less than the amount specified in the QDRO because it will be reduced by the amount withheld.

A distribution of a nontransferable annuity contract will not result in current recognition of income unless it is cashed in. Instead, the participant recognizes income as the annuity payments are received. However, if an endowment or life insurance contract is distributed, the entire cash value must be converted within 60 days to a nontransferable annuity contract in order to avoid current taxation.[209]

---

[206] IRS Notice 87-13, 1987-1 C.B. 432, Q&A 13.
[207] Code §§ 402(e)(1), 72(m)(10).
[208] IRS Notice 89-25, 1989-1 C.B. 662, Q&A 3.
[209] Treas. Reg. § 1.402(a)-1(a)(2).

Distributions as a result of the permanent loss or loss of use of a member or function of the body or permanent disfigurement may be excluded from income under § 105(c) of the Code, depending on the plan document and on how the amount distributed is determined.[210] Even if the plan is designated as a health benefit plan, the distribution may not be excludible from taxable income unless the amount of distribution is related to the permanent loss or loss of use of a member or function of the body or permanent disfigurement.[211]

C. Taxable Portion of Roth IRA Distributions

Qualified distributions from Roth IRAs are not subject to federal income tax.[212] A *qualified distribution* is one that meets a five-year holding period and is for one of several permitted purposes.[213] For distributions attributable to annual contributions to a Roth IRA, the five-year holding period is met if the distribution occurs after the end of the fifth tax year beginning with the first tax year for which an annual contribution was made to a Roth IRA established for the distributee.[214] For distributions properly attributable to an amount rolled over or converted from a traditional IRA, the five-year holding period begins with the tax year in which the rollover or conversion occurred.[215] The purpose prong of the qualified distribution definition is met if the individual has attained age 59½, has died or has become totally and permanently disabled, or if the distribution is a qualified first-time homebuyer distribution.[216]

If a Roth IRA distribution is not a qualified distribution, it is taxed to the extent that the current distribution plus all prior distributions exceed the aggregate amount of contributions to the Roth IRA.[217] Treating distributions as coming first from contributions is significantly simpler and, typically, more taxpayer-favorable than the pro rata basis recovery applicable to qualified retirement plans and traditional IRAs.

---

[210] *See, e.g., Wood v. United States,* 590 F.2d 321 (9th Cir. 1979); *Masterson* v. *United States,* 478 F. Supp. 454 (N.D. Ill. 1979).

[211] *See, e.g., Berman* v. *Commissioner,* 925 F.2d 936 (6th Cir. 1991), affirming the Tax Court, T.C. Memo 1989-654.

[212] Code § 408A(d)(1).

[213] Code § 408A(d)(2).

[214] Code § 408A(d)(2)(B).

[215] Code § 408A(d)(3)(F).

[216] Code §§ 408A(d)(2)(A), 72(m)(7), 72(t)(2)(F). *See* Section B of Chapter Two for the definition of a first-time homebuyer distribution.

[217] Code § 408A(d)(4)(B).

D. Qualifying for Lump Sum Treatment

Certain lump sum distributions may qualify for special averaging and capital gain treatment. Special averaging and capital gain treatment is available with respect to distributions from qualified retirement plans, but not from IRAs. A lump sum distribution is also eligible for rollover into an IRA or another qualified retirement plan. Other types of distributions may also qualify for a rollover and are described in Section H of this chapter.

Electing lump sum treatment also allows the recipient to defer tax on any net unrealized appreciation on employer securities. The treatment of net unrealized appreciation on employer securities is discussed in Section F of this chapter.

Under a provision that predates TRA 86, lump sum treatment is not available to the extent that the amount of the distribution to a participant who is a five percent owner exceeds the amount of the participant's accrued benefit determined under the plan's benefit formula.[218]

An alternate payee who is either the spouse or a former spouse of the participant is entitled to elect lump sum treatment with respect to a distribution under a QDRO if the distribution is the entire amount payable to the alternate payee under the QDRO.[219]

A *lump sum distribution* is a distribution, within one taxable year of the recipient (usually a calendar year), of the balance to the credit of a participant that becomes payable to the recipient:

(1) On account of the participant's death;

(2) After the participant attains age 59½;

(3) On account of the participant's separation from service, but only if the participant is not self-employed; or

(4) After the participant has become disabled, but only if the participant is self-employed.[220]

---

[218] Former Code §§ 402(d)(4)(G), 72(m)(5).
[219] Former Code § 402(d)(4)(J).
[220] Code § 402(e)(4)(D)(i).

A person is self-employed if he or she is either a partner in a partnership, a member of a limited liability company taxed as a partnership, or a sole proprietor.

The distinctions made with respect to self-employed persons have little continuing significance. First, most participants who are not self-employed and who become disabled usually would separate from service as a result of that disability and therefore would qualify for lump sum treatment because of the separation from service. Second, since a participant after 1986 may make only one election after reaching age 59½ to use special averaging, any participant who separates from service before reaching age 59½ will be unable to elect special averaging treatment. A participant who reached age 50 before 1986 and who is not self-employed may make the election before reaching age 59½ but will not be entitled to make another election thereafter.

If a participant separates from the service of the employer sponsoring the plan before reaching age 59½, a distribution from that plan after he or she reaches age 59½ that satisfies the other requirements for lump sum treatment will qualify for lump sum treatment.[221]

If a participant separates from service but continues to perform services on behalf of his or her former employer, the IRS usually will claim that the participant has not separated from service unless the participant has become substantively an independent contractor and the nature of his or her duties has changed.[222] Also, in the case of a merger, consolidation, or sale of assets, a participant will not be considered to have separated from service if the participant continues in the same position as an employee of the resulting or purchasing corporation.[223]

Although an annuity contract that is distributed as part of a distribution is not currently taxable to the recipient, the inclusion of such a contract in the distribution will not disqualify the balance of the distribution for lump sum treatment. However, for purposes of determining the tax on the lump sum distribution, the actuarial value of the annuity is added to the sum of

---

[221] Priv. Ltr. Rul. 9049047.

[222] *See Reinhardt v. Commissioner,* 85 T.C. 511 (1985); Rev. Rul. 69-647, 1969-2 C.B. 100.

[223] *See, e.g., Dickson v. Commissioner,* T.C. Memo 1990-177; *Edwards v. Commissioner,* T.C. Memo 1989-409. *See also* Rev. Rul. 79-336, 1979-2 C.B. 187.

cash and the value of other property distributed.[224] The actual tax that is payable with respect to the current distribution is then determined by subtracting the tax computed on the actuarial value of the annuity from the tax computed on the value of the entire amount distributed, including the actuarial value of the annuity. When distributions under the annuity contract are actually received, they are taxed as ordinary income, in the manner described in Section B of this chapter.

The participant may make only one election to use five-year averaging and only after the participant has reached age 59½.[225] A transition rule, discussed in the next section, gives a participant who reached age 50 before January 1, 1986, the option of using ten-year averaging instead. Such a participant may also elect capital gain treatment for the portion of the distribution deemed to be attributable to participation before 1974. Although the participant may elect special averaging or capital gain treatment even if he or she has not reached age 59½, the distribution may be subject to the 10 percent penalty on premature distributions unless an exception applies. Averaging may also be elected by an individual beneficiary, an estate, or a trust receiving the benefit of a participant who had reached age 59½ before his or her death (or age 50 before 1986 in the case of the transition rule).[226]

The Small Business Act repealed five-year averaging for taxable years after 1999, but retained the transition rule allowing participants who reached age 50 on January 1, 1986, to use ten-year averaging and capital gain treatment.[227]

For purposes of determining the balance to the credit of the account of a participant, all trusts that are part of a plan are treated as a single trust.[228] Under this rule, all pension plans (including money purchase pension plans) maintained by the same employer are treated as a single plan; all profit-sharing plans maintained by the same employer are treated as a single plan; and all stock bonus plans maintained by the same employer are treated as a single plan. Employers that are members of a controlled group of corporations are treated as a single employer. Trusts that are not

---

[224] Former Code §§ 402(d)(2)(A), (C).

[225] Code § 402(e)(4)(B).

[226] *Id.*, as amended by TAMRA § 1011A(b)(6).

[227] The Small Business Act § 1401.

[228] Code § 402(e)(4)(D)(ii).

qualified under Code § 401(a) or § 403 (such as nonqualified deferred compensation plans and nonqualified annuity contracts) are disregarded.

If a participant who separates from service receives the balance to the credit of his or her account, the potential increased vesting in his or her accrued benefit if he or she is rehired by the same employer will not disqualify the original distribution for special averaging.[229] However, if the participant is rehired by the same employer and as a result increases his or her vested interest in the benefit accrued before the separation, under either the distributing plan or any plan required to be aggregated with the distributing plan, the tax saved by using special averaging will be recaptured. In this case, the previous election will not preclude the participant from making a later election to use special averaging for a distribution from any plan, including the distributing plan.[230]

Distributions to the participant before his or her death will not preclude the participant's beneficiary from electing lump sum treatment with respect to a distribution of the balance of the benefit.[231]

In order for a participant to elect special averaging, the participant must have participated in the plan for five or more taxable years before the taxable year in which the lump sum distribution is received.[232] If a participant's benefit is transferred directly from one plan to another, the participant's participation in the transferring plan can be tacked onto the participant's participation in the receiving plan,[233] but only if the entire balance is transferred.[234] Tacking will not apply if the funds are "rolled over" rather than being transferred between the trustees.[235] Presumably, a "direct rollover" that is mechanically transferred between plan trustees will receive the same treatment as a rollover that passes through the control of the participant, since the participant exercised rights to receive a distribution.[236] A year of participation under the five-year participation requirement does not include years in which contributions are not made to

---

[229] Former Code § 402(e)(6)(A).
[230] Former Code § 402(e)(6)(B).
[231] Prop. Reg. § 1.402(e)-2(d)(1)(ii)(B).
[232] Former Code § 402(e)(4)(H).
[233] Priv. Ltr. Rul. 8535059.
[234] Priv. Ltr. Rul. 8722110.
[235] Priv. Ltr. Rul. 8246103.
[236] Rev. Rul. 94-76,1994-2 C.B. 46.

a profit-sharing or stock bonus plan.[237] The five-year participation requirement does not apply to beneficiaries of a participant, who may elect averaging even if the deceased participant had less than five years of participation at death.[238]

The participant may not elect special averaging or capital gain treatment after the participant has rolled any part of a distribution into an IRA or another qualified retirement plan.[239] If a participant is not sure whether to elect special averaging or roll the distribution into an IRA or another qualified retirement plan, the participant can avoid the start of the 60-day period within which a rollover must be made by delaying the receipt of the distribution until the decision is made.

If there are multiple recipients, each recipient may elect special averaging independently of the other recipients, but each recipient electing special averaging pays a pro rata portion of the tax determined on the entire amount of the distribution.[240] Since a surviving spouse may roll a distribution of the decedent's benefit into an IRA (or, after 2001, another qualified retirement plan in which he or she is a participant),[241] he or she may not want to use special averaging, while other recipients, who may be unable to use a rollover, may want to use special averaging. However, as a result of the Pension Protection Act, a nonspouse beneficiary may be able to have the benefit transferred to an inherited IRA and take advantage of the life expectancy method of determining the required minimum distribution.[242]

E. Special Averaging and Capital Gain Treatment

Under five-year averaging, a qualifying lump sum distribution is taxed separately from the other income of the recipient.[243] The amount of tax is determined by multiplying by five the amount of tax, using the single taxpayer rate, on one-fifth of the excess of the total taxable amount of the lump sum distribution over the minimum distribution allowance.[244] The

---

[237] Priv. Ltr. Rul. 8110050.
[238] Prop. Reg. § 1.402(e)-2(e)(3).
[239] Temp. Reg. § 1.402(a)(5)-IT, Q&A 4.
[240] *See* Instructions to Form 4972, Tax on Lump Sum Distributions.
[241] TRA 2001 § 641(d), amending Code § 402(c)(9).
[242] See Chapter 2, C.6 for a discussion of the nonspousal rollover.
[243] Former Code § 402(d)(1). As discussed earlier, five-year averaging was repealed by the Small Business Act for taxable years after 1999.
[244] Former Code § 402(d)(1)(B).

minimum distribution allowance is equal to the lesser of $10,000 or one-half of the total taxable amount of the lump sum distribution for the taxable year, reduced (but not below zero) by 20 percent of the amount (if any) by which the total taxable amount exceeds $20,000.[245] Once the total taxable amount reaches $70,000, the minimum distribution allowance is eliminated ($10,000 – 20 percent × ($70,000 – $20,000) = 0). The total taxable amount includes the actuarial value of any annuity contracts that are part of the distribution, and is reduced by the participant's basis in the plan.

For example, assume a lump sum distribution of $50,000 to a participant who has not made any nondeductible contributions to the plan and has no other basis in the plan. The total taxable amount of $50,000 is reduced by the minimum distribution allowance of $4,000. The allowance is determined by reducing the lesser of $10,000 or one-half of the total taxable amount by 20 percent of the excess of the total taxable amount over $20,000. Twenty percent of $30,000 (the excess of the total taxable amount over 20,000) is $6,000; $10,000 (the lesser of $10,000 or one-half the total taxable amount) minus $6,000 is $4,000, which is the minimum distribution allowance. The balance after reducing the total taxable amount by $4,000 is $46,000 ($50,000 –$4,000), which is then divided by five. The result, $9,200, is the amount on which the initial tax is determined. The tax on $9,200 at the single taxpayer rate in 2015 (15 percent) is $1,380. This amount is then multiplied by five to arrive at the actual tax to be paid on the lump sum, which is $6,900. This tax is added to the recipient's other income tax for the year, which is determined without including the taxable amount of the lump sum distribution.

If there are multiple beneficiaries, each beneficiary may elect whether to take special averaging treatment or, if the participant's spouse is the beneficiary, he or she may roll the distribution into an IRA. If two or more trusts are beneficiaries, then the tax is apportioned according to the relative amount that each trust receives.[246]

Ten-year averaging, which applied before 1987, was determined by multiplying by ten the tax, using the single taxpayer rate, on one-tenth of the total taxable amount of the lump sum distribution over the minimum distribution allowance. An additional $2,300 was added to the amount on

---

[245] Former Code § 402(d)(1)(C).

[246] Former Code § 402(e)(2).

which the initial tax was calculated to take into account the zero bracket amount.[247]

Before 1987, capital gain treatment was available for the portion of the lump sum distribution attributable to years of participation before 1974.[248] The amount attributable to participation before 1974 was determined by multiplying the total distribution by a fraction. The numerator of the fraction was the number of months of participation before 1974. The denominator of the fraction was the total number of months of participation. In figuring months of active participation before 1974, any part of a calendar year in which the employee was a participant is counted as 12 months. In figuring months of active participation after 1973, any part of a calendar month the employee was a participant is counted as one month. Consequently, partial years of participation before 1974 are given more weight than partial years after 1973, thereby increasing the capital gain portion in some instances.

A transition rule applied to participants who had attained age 50 before January 1, 1986. Under this rule, a participant could make a one-time election either before or after attaining age 59½ to use five-year averaging (under the new tax rates) or ten-year averaging (using the 1986 rates).[249] In addition, such a participant could elect capital gain treatment at a 20 percent rate with respect to the portion of the lump sum distribution that would have qualified for long-term capital gain treatment before 1987. The election under this transition rule could also be made by an individual beneficiary, trust, or estate of a deceased participant if the participant reached age 50 before January 1, 1986.[250]

F. Employer Securities

For income tax purposes, a participant may postpone the recognition of gain on any net unrealized appreciation in any employer securities received as part of a distribution from a qualified retirement plan. If the distribution does not qualify as a lump sum distribution, the net unrealized appreciation in employer securities attributable to nondeductible employee contributions to the plan is excludible from the recipient's gross income in the year of distribution.[251] If a distribution qualifies as a lump sum

[247] Code § 402(e)(1)(C), before amendment by TRA 86 §§ 1122(a)(2)(A), (B).
[248] Code § 402(e)(4)(E), before repeal by TRA 86 § 1122(b)(2)(D).
[249] TRA 86 §§ 1122(h)(3), (5), (6).
[250] TAMRA § 1011A(b)(15), amending TRA 86 § 1122(h)(5).
[251] Code § 402(e)(4)(A).

distribution, all net unrealized appreciation in employer securities, whether attributable to employer or employee contributions, is excludible from gross income.[252] The five-year participation requirement that must be satisfied to elect special averaging need not be satisfied to obtain this treatment. If the participant rolls the distribution into an IRA, subsequent distributions from the IRA will not qualify for the deferral, since lump sum treatment is not available for distributions from IRAs.[253]

Net unrealized appreciation is the difference between the market value of employer securities at the time of the distribution and the cost or other basis of the securities to the plan.[254] If the securities were contributed to the plan by the sponsoring corporation, the basis is the fair market value at the time of the contribution. The term *employer securities* means shares of stock, bonds, or debentures issued with interest coupons or in registered form by the employer corporation that sponsors the plan or a parent or subsidiary of the employer corporation.[255] The basis of the plan in employer securities involved in certain exchanges, as well as dispositions and reacquisitions completed within 90 days, does not change for purposes of determining the amount of net unrealized appreciation.[256]

Effective for distributions received after December 31, 1986, a taxpayer receiving a lump sum distribution may elect on the return on which the distribution is required to be included in income not to have the net unrealized appreciation excluded from the taxable part of the distribution.[257] If the election is made, the income recognized and the recipient's basis in the securities is equal to the fair market value of the securities at the date of distribution. If the total amount of the lump sum distribution is small, taxing net unrealized appreciation under special ten-year averaging or as capital gains may result in a lower tax than deferring the tax until a later disposition of the securities.

The amount of net unrealized appreciation is taxable as long-term capital gain to the extent recognized in a subsequent disposition of the securities.[258] Any recognized gain in excess of the net unrealized appreciation is taxable

---

[252] Code § 402(e)(4)(B).
[253] Code § 408(d).
[254] Treas. Reg. § 1.402(a)-1(b)(2)(i).
[255] Code § 402(e)(4)(E).
[256] Code § 402(j).
[257] Code § 402(e)(4)(B).
[258] Prop. Reg. § 1.402(a)-1(b)(1)(i).

either as short-term or long-term capital gain, depending on how long the recipient held the securities.[259] If a beneficiary of the recipient sells the securities, the net unrealized appreciation is treated as income in respect of a decedent (IRD).[260]

If the value of a lump sum distribution of employer securities is less than the amount the participant contributed to the plan, no loss is recognized at the time of the distribution.[261] Instead, the basis of the securities for determining gain on resale would be the amount of employee contributions, and the loss will be recognized at that time. The loss will be treated as a miscellaneous itemized deduction.[262]

If a rollover is made that does not qualify for deferral treatment under Code § 402(c), the net unrealized appreciation attributable to the securities purchased with employee contributions will be currently taxable.[263] Prior to 2002, a distribution of employer securities from a qualified plan could not be rolled into an IRA in order to avoid current taxation because nondeductible employee contributions could not be rolled into an IRA. However, since the participant may elect to allocate his or her nondeductible contributions to cash and other property in any manner he or she wishes,[264] the recognition of any income with respect to the securities rolled into an IRA can be deferred if the participant allocates his or her nondeductible contributions to cash or property other than the distributed employer securities. The securities (or the proceeds from a sale of the securities, including any gain realized) may then be rolled into a traditional IRA, deferring the gain until a later distribution.

For an example of how the deferral works, assume that a plan purchases qualifying employer securities in 2001 for $100 a share. Assume that a lump sum distribution is made to a participant in 2006 when the value of the securities is $150 a share. The participant would be taxable to the extent of $100 a share (the basis of the plan in the securities) and he or she would have a basis in the securities of $100 a share. Regardless of when the participant sells the securities, the net unrealized appreciation per share not taxed at the time of the distribution will be treated as long-term

---

[259] *Id.*

[260] Rev. Rul. 69-297, 1969-1 C.B. 131.

[261] Rev. Rul. 71-251, 1971-1 C.B. 129.

[262] Rev. Rul. 72-305, 1972-1 C.B. 116.

[263] *See* Code §§ 402(e)(4)(A), (c).

[264] Code § 402(c)(6)(C).

capital gain to the extent of the unrealized appreciation at the date of distribution ($50 in this case), but only to the extent gain is recognized on the sale. If the participant sells the securities for more than $150 a share, any additional gain will be short- or long-term capital gain, depending upon the holding period of the participant after the distribution. If the participant sells the securities for less than $100 a share (for example, at $80 per share), he or she will have a long-term capital loss of $20 per share.

G. Income in Respect of a Decedent

The taxable amount of distributions received by an estate or beneficiary of a deceased participant from qualified retirement plans and IRAs is treated as IRD under Code § 691. Consequently, there is no step-up in basis under Code § 1014 with respect to such amounts. The recipient reports the entire taxable amount received as ordinary income in the year received unless there has been a previous taxable disposition of the right to the benefits. When a qualified disclaimer has been used, the actual recipient of the benefit, and not the disclaiming person, will have IRD.[265]

If there is a taxable disposition of the right to the benefits, such as a transfer pursuant to a pecuniary bequest, then the estate will recognize current income equal to the present value of the benefits and the transferee will have a basis equal to the amount of income recognized by the estate.[266] Consequently, qualified retirement plan benefits and IRAs should not be used to satisfy a pecuniary bequest, including a pecuniary marital deduction formula bequest. A specific bequest of the qualified retirement plan benefits or IRAs or the use of a fractional share marital deduction formula will avoid the current recognition of taxable income. However, some commentators believe that income should not be recognized when a plan benefit or IRA is used to satisfy a pecuniary bequest, because a recipient only includes the benefit or IRA in gross income when it is actually received.[267] A Chief Counsel Advice has taken the position that the satisfaction of a pecuniary bequest to a charitable organization with an interest in an IRA results in current recognition of income and no offsetting charitable deduction.[268]

---

265 Priv. Ltr. Rul. 9630034.

266 Code § 691(a)(2); Treas. Reg. § 1.661(a)-2(f)(1).

267 Code §§ 402(a), 408(d)(1), 408A(d)(1).

268 Chief Counsel Advice (CCA) 200644020.

The recipient, whether the estate or another beneficiary, is entitled to a deduction for the estate tax paid with respect to the benefits (the IRD deduction). The amount of the deduction available to a recipient for a taxable year is determined by multiplying the estate tax attributable to all items of IRD by a fraction. The numerator of the fraction is the amount of IRD that is included in the recipient's gross income for the taxable year. The denominator of the fraction is the total amount of IRD included in the decedent's federal gross estate, less any expenses deductible from the gross estate attributable to the IRD.[269] The estate tax attributable to all items of IRD is the excess of the estate tax computed including IRD over the estate tax computed excluding IRD.[270] Although the IRD deduction must be taken as an itemized deduction and is subject to the 3 percent reduction under Code § 68, it is not subject to the 2 percent floor on miscellaneous itemized deductions.[271]

If the benefit is specifically given to the spouse or to a trust for the benefit of the spouse that qualifies for the marital deduction, there will be no IRD deduction since the estate tax is the same with or without the inclusion of the benefit. If the benefit is excluded from the gross estate, it not only reduces the gross estate but also reduces the marital deduction on a dollar-for-dollar basis, resulting in the same taxable amount. If the marital deduction is funded pursuant to a formula that depends upon the value of the gross estate, then there will be a deduction for IRD purposes if there is an estate tax payable, since the exclusion of the benefit from the gross estate does not reduce the marital deduction on a dollar-for-dollar basis. If the unlimited marital deduction is being used to reduce the estate tax to zero, there will be no IRD deduction since there will be no estate tax.

For example, assume a gross estate of $20,000,000 after deductions for administration expenses, but before the marital deduction. Assume that part of this amount is $2,000,000 of plan benefits and there is no other IRD. Assume also that there is a formula bequest to the spouse that qualifies for the marital deduction equal to one-fourth of the gross estate after administration expenses, or $5,000,000. As long as plan benefits are not specifically bequeathed to the spouse, the IRD deduction would be $600,000: the excess of the estate tax on $15,000,000 (the taxable estate including the IRD, but excluding the $5,000,000 marital deduction), which

---

[269] Code §§ 691(c)(1), (2)(B).
[270] Code § 691(c)(2)(C).
[271] Code § 67(b)(8).

is $3,828,000, over the estate tax on $13,500,000 (the taxable estate after excluding the IRD and the marital deduction, now only $4,500,000, one-fourth of $18,000,000), which is $3,228,000. Note that the IRD deduction is exactly 40 percent of the difference in the taxable estate including the IRD and the taxable estate excluding the IRD.

Proceeds of a life insurance policy held by a qualified retirement plan that are paid to the estate or beneficiaries of a deceased participant in excess of any cash value of the policy are excluded from income tax under Code § 101(a), but only if the economic value of the life insurance coverage (the P.S. 58 cost) has either been paid by nondeductible employee contributions or is taxable to the participant.[272]

Before August 21, 1996, Code § 101(b) excluded up to $5,000 of any death benefit paid by the employer to the estate or beneficiaries of a deceased employee from the recipient's gross income. The $5,000 exclusion was allocated among beneficiaries in proportion to the beneficiaries' shares of the distribution. The exclusion only applied if the decedent's right to receive the benefit while living was forfeitable, unless the benefit was part of a lump sum distribution satisfying the requirements described in Section D of this chapter.[273] In the case of a sole proprietor or partner, the $5,000 death benefit exclusion only applied to distributions from qualified retirement plans.[274] The exclusion did not apply to a beneficiary entitled to receive benefits under a joint and survivor annuity if the deceased participant had already begun receiving payments under the annuity prior to death.[275]

If other payments were received from the employer that also qualified for the $5,000 exclusion, the entire exclusion could have been allocated to the other payments if special averaging or capital gain treatment was elected for the distribution from the qualified retirement plan. By allocating the exclusion to other benefits, the exclusion would have been used more efficiently to reduce income not eligible for special tax treatment.[276]

---

[272] Code § 72(m)(3)(C); Treas. Reg. § 1.72-16(c)(2)(ii), (4).

[273] Former Code § 101(b)(2)(B).

[274] Former Code § 101(b)(3)(B).

[275] Former Code § 101(b)(2)(C).

[276] *See Estate of W. R. Olsen,* T.C. Memo 1961-161, *rev'd on other grounds,* 302 F.2d 671 (8th Cir. 1962).

H. Rollovers to Traditional IRAs

A participant, and in certain cases the participant's spouse, may elect to roll some or all of a qualifying distribution from a qualified retirement plan into a traditional IRA. A rollover permits the participant or spouse to defer the payment of income tax on the distribution until the participant either needs the benefits for living expenses or other personal reasons or must begin receiving distributions under the minimum distribution rules discussed in Section C of Chapter Two. By rolling the distribution into a traditional IRA, the payment of the income tax is deferred, allowing the participant to continue to invest the deferred income tax. In addition, the funds, including the deferred income tax, continue to earn income on a tax-deferred basis.

To qualify for a rollover, all or part of the amount qualifying for rollover treatment must be transferred to a traditional IRA or another qualified retirement plan within 60 days after receipt.[277] The amount rolled over will not be includible in the gross income of the recipient for the taxable year in which paid. Although the entire distribution need not be rolled over, the portion not rolled over will be subject to ordinary income tax. The maximum amount that may be rolled over is the sum of cash and other property distributed, less the amount of nondeductible employee contributions included in the distribution unless the rollover is to an IRA or is a direct rollover to a qualified retirement plan that agrees to separately account for such amounts.[278]

If the distribution includes property, the property or the proceeds from the sale of the property may be rolled over.[279] Any gain or loss realized on the sale of property will not be recognized provided that the post-distribution gain is rolled over.[280] However, a participant may not keep noncash property received in a distribution and roll an equivalent amount of cash into the traditional IRA or another qualified retirement plan.[281] Although a life insurance policy that is part of a distribution from a qualified plan may not be rolled into an IRA (because the Code prohibits the holding of a life insurance policy in an IRA), the policy may be cashed in and the proceeds rolled into an IRA.[282]

---

[277] Code §§ 402(c)(1), (3).
[278] Code § 402(c)(2).
[279] Code §S 402(c)(1)(C), (6).
[280] Code § 402(c)(6)(D).
[281] Rev. Rul. 87-77, 1987-2 C.B. 115.
[282] Code § 408(a)(3).

The 60-day rule has been strictly construed by the IRS. The 60-day period commences with the physical receipt of the distribution.[283] Generally, no extension will be granted.[284] If more than one distribution is made during the same taxable year, the 60-day period commences on the date on which the last payment is received.[285] However, effective for distributions after 2001, the IRS is authorized to waive the 60-day requirement where the failure to do so would be against equity or good conscience, including casualty, disaster, or other events beyond the reasonable control of the individual subject to such requirement.[286]

In *Michel* v. *Commissioner,*[287] the taxpayer transferred a distribution from a qualified retirement plan into an IRA after the 60-day period had expired. The Tax Court agreed with the IRS that although the taxpayer missed the 60-day deadline, a valid IRA was nonetheless established, thereby subjecting the taxpayer to a 6 percent penalty for an excess contribution to an IRA in addition to ordinary income tax on the distribution itself. In *Wood* v. *Commissioner,*[288] the Tax Court allowed a rollover when the taxpayer had done everything to satisfy the 60-day rule, but the account was not properly established because of a clerical error by an employee of the IRA sponsor.

The 60-day period does not include any period during which the amount of the distribution is frozen in a financial institution because of the bankruptcy or insolvency of the financial institution, and the 60-day period will not end earlier than ten days after the amount ceases to be frozen.[289]

Before 1993, there were four types of distributions that qualified for rollover treatment: a lump sum distribution, a distribution due to the termination of the plan, a distribution of more than 50 percent of a participant's balance (a "partial distribution"), and a distribution of accumulated deductible employee contributions, which were permitted under the law before 1986.[290]

---

[283] Priv. Ltr. Ruls. 8804014 and 8833043.
[284] Priv. Ltr. Ruls. 8548073 and 8608049.
[285] Priv. Ltr. Rul. 8604092.
[286] TRA 2001 § 644, amending Code § 402(c)(3).
[287] T.C. Memo 1989-670.
[288] 93 T.C. 114 (1989).
[289] Code § 402(c)(7).
[290] Former Code §§ 402(a)(5)(B), (E)(i), (E)(v).

The Unemployment Compensation Amendments of 1992 substantially changed the rules that applied to rollovers. After 1992, any distribution from a qualified retirement plan (including annuities described in Code §§ 403(a) and 403(b)) is eligible for rollover treatment except:

(1) A distribution that is one of a series of substantially equal periodic payments (not less frequently than annually) for the life or life expectancy of the employee or the joint lives or joint life expectancies of the employee and the employee's designated beneficiary or for a specified period of ten years or more;

(2) Any distribution to the extent that the distribution is required under the minimum distribution rules contained in Code § 401(a)(9);

(3) Corrective distributions of elective deferrals, after-tax employee contributions, and matching contributions;

(4) Participant loans treated as deemed distributions because they exceed one of the size, maturity, or amortization limits;

(5) Dividends on employer stock;

(6) The cost of life insurance coverage; and

(7) The portion of any distribution that consists of after-tax employee contributions.[291]

A qualified retirement or annuity plan must now permit participants to elect to have any distribution that is eligible for rollover treatment transferred in a "direct rollover" to a qualified retirement plan or traditional IRA specified by the participant.[292] In addition, withholding is imposed at the rate of 20 percent on any distribution that is eligible to be rolled over but is not transferred directly to a qualified retirement plan or traditional IRA, regardless of whether the recipient intends to roll over the distribution.[293] Qualified retirement plans have been encouraged to accept rollover contributions by IRS assurance that accepting such contributions based on reasonable evidence that the distributing plan was qualified will not

[291] Code §§ 402, 403, as amended by DCA § 521(a); Treas. Reg. §§ 1.402(c)-2, Q&A-4, 1.403(b)-2, Q&A-1.

[292] DCA § 522(a)(I), adding Code § 401(a)(31).

[293] DCA § 522(b)(1), amending Code § 3405 by adding new subsection (c).

disqualify the receiving plan if the distributing plan, in fact, turns out not to have been qualified.[294]

A spouse of a deceased participant may roll over some or all of a distribution of the decedent's plan benefit to an IRA and after 2001, to another qualified plan or qualified annuity.[295] A spouse may also elect to treat the IRA of the deceased spouse as his or her own IRA.[296] The IRS, in a private letter ruling, permitted a spouse to use a spousal rollover even though the spouse was not the designated beneficiary because the benefits were payable to the decedent's estate and the spouse was the sole beneficiary of the estate.[297] Another private letter ruling permitted a spousal rollover for benefits payable to a trust that was revocable by the surviving spouse and provided that its assets were distributable to the spouse in the event of revocation.[298]

A surviving spouse who is the beneficiary of a deceased participant's benefit from a qualified retirement plan may have an additional option that is not available to other beneficiaries. If, under the terms of the plan, the spouse is entitled to a lump sum distribution, the spouse may roll over that distribution into an IRA in the name of the deceased participant for which the spouse is the beneficiary.[299] This option may be more favorable than rolling over to the surviving spouse's IRA if the deceased participant was younger than the surviving spouse, because distributions may be delayed until the participant would have attained age 70½ or if the surviving spouse will be taking distributions prior to reaching age 59½ and would be subject to the 10 percent premature withdrawal penalty. The option may be preferable to leaving the balance in the qualified plan if an IRA gives the spouse greater investment and distribution flexibility.

A distribution to a spouse or former spouse of a participant who is an alternate payee under a QDRO may be rolled into the spouse's IRA or qualified retirement plan in which the spouse or former spouse is a participant under the same requirements that apply to a participant or

---

[294] Rev. Rul. 96-48, I.R.B. 1996-40. TRA 97 § 1509 directs the Treasury to clarify that a determination letter with respect to the transferring plan is not necessary in order for the administrator to conclude that the rollover is valid.

[295] Code § 402(c)(9).

[296] Treas. Reg. § 1.408-8, A-5(a).

[297] Priv. Ltr. Rul. 8746055.

[298] Priv. Ltr. Rul. 8920045.

[299] Priv. Ltr. Ruls. 9608042 and 9418034.

former participant in the distributing plan.[300] No recipient other than a spouse of a deceased participant or a spouse or former spouse who is an alternate payee under a QDRO may roll a distribution of a decedent's benefit into an IRA or another qualified retirement plan. A federal district court, however, has upheld the right of the estate of a decedent to roll over a distribution the decedent received within 60 days of his or her death.[301]

If certain requirements are met, a participant may roll a distribution from a conduit IRA into another qualified retirement plan, thereby preserving special averaging or capital gain treatment. To take advantage of this rule, some or all of a qualified total distribution from a qualified retirement plan must be rolled into one or more traditional IRAs and the participant may not make any additional contributions to the traditional IRA if it is to qualify as a conduit IRA. If the participant subsequently receives a distribution from such an IRA, the participant then may roll some or all of the distribution into a qualified retirement plan within 60 days after receipt. The receiving plan must be the same type of plan as the original plan. For this purpose, plans under Code §§ 401(a) and 403(a) are treated as the same type of plan and are different from plans qualified under Code § 403(b), which are tax-sheltered annuities for employees of tax-exempt organizations or public school systems.[302]

As a result of TRA 2001, effective for distributions after 2001, rollovers may be made between qualified retirement plans, 403(b) annuity plans, and Section 457 plans. A separate account must be established for transfers from a qualified retirement plan or a 403(b) annuity plan to a Section 457 plan to ensure that distributions of such amounts are identifiable for purposes of the 10 percent additional income tax on distributions before age 59½ that applies to qualified retirement plans and 403(b) annuities, but not to Section 457 plans. Because of the expanded rollover rules, plans are now required to provide expanded explanations to recipients of eligible rollover distributions concerning restrictions and tax consequences that apply to plans to which the participant may make a rollover that are different from those applicable to distributions from a plan making the distribution.[303]

[300] Code § 402(e)(1)(B).
[301] *Gunther v. United States*, 573 F. Supp. 126 (W.D. Mich. 1982).
[302] Code § 408(d)(3)(A).
[303] TRA 2001 § 641, amending Code §§ 457, 402, 403(b).

Before 2002, a deceased participant's spouse receiving a distribution as a beneficiary could not use a conduit IRA to transfer the decedent's benefits to another qualified retirement plan.[304] Effective for distributions after 2001, the surviving spouse of a deceased participant in a qualified retirement plan may make a tax-free rollover of an eligible rollover distribution to another qualified retirement plan, a 403(b) annuity, or a Section 457 plan in which the spouse participates, as well as to an IRA, which was already permitted.[305]

A rollover from one traditional IRA to another traditional IRA or from a traditional IRA to a qualified retirement plan or annuity may not be made if the recipient made another rollover during the one-year period ending on the date of receipt of the second distribution.[306] For rollovers before January 1, 2015, this rule applied separately to each IRA maintained by the same participant. However, because of a Tax Court case decided in 2014,[307] the IRS issued Announcement 2014-15, which provided that, beginning with rollovers occurring after 2014, an individual cannot make an IRA-to-IRA rollover if he or she made such a rollover involving any of the individual's IRAs in the preceding one-year period. Transfers from one traditional IRA directly into another traditional IRA are not rollovers, since the participant never has control over the distribution.[308] Consequently, transfers from one traditional IRA to another traditional IRA may be made as frequently as the participant desires.

TRA 2001, effective for distributions after 2001, permits a distribution from an IRA to be rolled into a qualified retirement plan, a 403(b) annuity, or a Section 457 plan, if the entire amount received (including money and any other property), but not exceeding the portion of the amount received which is includable in gross income, is paid into an eligible retirement plan for the benefit of the individual not later than the 60th day after the date on which the payment or distribution is received. Put another way, only deductible contributions to an IRA and earnings on all contributions may be rolled into such plans.[309] In addition, effective for distributions made after 2001, after-tax contributions to a qualified retirement plan may be rolled over to another qualified retirement plan or IRA. A rollover of

---

[304] Code § 408(d)(3)(B), prior to amendment by UCA 92.

[305] TRA 2001 § 641(d), amending Code § 402(c)(9).

[306] Code § 408(d)(3)(B); Prop. Reg. § 1.408-4(b)(4)(ii).

[307] *Bobrow v. Commissioner*, T.C. Memo 2014-21.

[308] Rev. Rul. 78-406, 1978-2 C.B. 157.

[309] TRA 2001 § 642, amending Code § 408(d)(3).

after-tax contributions from a qualified retirement plan to another qualified retirement plan can only be carried out through a direct trustee-to-trustee transfer, and the transferee qualified retirement plan must separately track the contributions and any related earnings. Note that after-tax contributions may not be rolled over from an IRA to a qualified retirement plan, 403(b) annuity, or Section 457 deferred compensation plan.[310]

The IRS has ruled that a person may use funds received from an IRA for personal needs during the 60-day period without jeopardizing the tax-free rollover, as long as the funds are redeposited into an IRA before the end of the 60-day period.[311]

Once any portion of a total distribution is irrevocably designated as a rollover contribution, the distribution is not eligible for special averaging and capital gain treatment.[312] As a result, a participant cannot withdraw funds that were previously deposited into an IRA in an attempt to qualify the distribution for special averaging or capital gain treatment, regardless of when the withdrawal from the IRA is made.

As mentioned in Chapter Two, a required minimum distribution received pursuant to the minimum distribution rules after a person reaches his or her RBD may not be rolled into an IRA.[313]

I. Rollovers to Roth IRAs

Rollovers and transfers can be made from one Roth IRA to another in, generally, the same manner as described in Section H for traditional IRAs.[314]

Under certain circumstances, rollovers may also be allowed from a traditional IRA to a Roth IRA.[315] Before 2010, such rollovers could only be made if the individual was either a single person or a married person filing a joint tax return and the individual's or married couple's modified

[310] TRA 2001 § 643, amending Code §§ 402(c), 401(a)(31), 408(d).
[311] Priv. Ltr. Rul. 9010007.
[312] Treas. Reg. § 1.402(a)(5)-1T, Q&A 4.
[313] Code §§ 402(c)(4)(B), 408(d)(3)(E).
[314] Code §§ 408A(a), 408(d)(3).
[315] *Id.*

AGI did not exceed $100,000.[316] Stated conversely, a married person filing separately with any amount of income and a single person or joint filer with income exceeding $100,000 may not make a traditional IRA to Roth IRA rollover.

The Pension Protection Act of 2006 (PPA) permits rollovers from a qualified plan directly to a Roth IRA. Effective for distributions after December 31, 2007, a distribution from a tax-qualified retirement plan, tax-sheltered annuity, or governmental 457 plan may be rolled over directly from such plan into a Roth IRA. The amount rolled over in excess of any nondeductible contributions made to the plan is included in gross income and. As mentioned, before 2010 such a rollover was not available to an individual with adjusted gross income of $100,000 or more. After 2009, as a result of the 2005 Tax Increase Prevention and Reconciliation Act,[317] which amended § 408A to eliminate the income limits on conversions of traditional IRAs to Roth IRAs,[318] any individual, regardless of his or her AGI, may roll over amounts from traditional IRAs and eligible retirement plans to a Roth IRA. If the conversion or rollover took place in 2010, the individual recognized 50% of the income in 2011 and the balance in 2012. However, if the account holder received a distribution in 2010 or 2011 from the Roth IRA, income was recognized to the extent the distribution exceeded the amount that would have otherwise been includible in income under the deferral provision. As a result of the new rule, a participant in a qualified retirement plan or other tax-favored plan will not have to roll over a distribution to a traditional IRA in order to roll the same amount into a Roth IRA. With the elimination of the income limitation after 2009, every individual who is either an account holder of a traditional IRA or a participant in a qualified retirement plan will need to consider whether to convert the existing traditional IRA to a Roth IRA or to roll the qualified retirement plan benefit into a Roth IRA.

The ability to roll a benefit directly from a qualified retirement plan to a Roth IRA not only eliminates a step in achieving a Roth IRA conversion, but may also allow more of the amount rolled over to be treated as after-tax contributions not subject to income tax, thereby reducing the tax cost of the rollover. Under the normal rules regarding distributions from IRAs, any distribution, including a rollover, will be treated as a pro rata portion

---

[316] Code § 408A(c)(3)(B).

[317] Pub. L. No. 109-222, § 512(a).

[318] *See* § 408A(c)(3), as amended by the 2005 Tax Increase Prevention and Reconciliation Act, Pub. L. No. 109-222, § 512(a).

of before-tax and after-tax contributions to all the participant's IRAs. Consequently, a participant in a qualified retirement plan who has made substantial after-tax contributions to the plan would want to avoid having the plan benefit aggregated with his or her traditional IRAs if they consist of mostly before-tax contributions. A direct rollover of the qualified plan benefit to a Roth IRA would avoid aggregating the plan benefit with the participant's traditional IRAs in determining the amount of before-tax and after-tax contributions.

After 2005, a Roth IRA may be rolled into a Roth designated account that is part of a qualified retirement plan and vice versa.[319]

[319] TRA 2001 § 617, adding Code § 402A.

Chapter Four

Transfer Taxes

A. Gift Taxation

Before 1987, Code § 2517 excluded from taxable gifts a transfer of an interest in a qualified retirement plan benefit or IRA. As a result of TRA 86, an irrevocable election by a participant or any failure of a participant to act, either of which results in any part of his or her plan benefit or IRA being irrevocably payable to someone else, is treated as a taxable gift.[320] Unless the beneficiary has a present interest in the benefit (the beneficiary is immediately entitled to the benefit payment), the gift will not qualify for the annual exclusion. Because of the nonalienation requirement under Code § 401(a)(13) applicable to qualified retirement plans, the only way that a plan benefit may be payable to a beneficiary before the participant retires is pursuant to a QDRO. A payment pursuant to a QDRO is not a taxable gift. After the participant retires, he or she may make a revocable assignment of up to 10 percent of his or her benefit. In this case, the annual gift tax exclusion should be available when the payments are actually made to the assignee (when the gift becomes complete). An assignment of all or part of an IRA will cause the account holder to recognize taxable income on the amount of the IRA assigned.[321]

The waiver of a survivor benefit to which a participant's spouse is entitled under REA will not be treated as a transfer of property by gift.[322] Nontaxable treatment may not apply to the nonparticipant spouse's community property interest in the benefit to which he or she is entitled under a state's community property laws, although in most cases the value of the spouse's rights under REA will equal or exceed his or her community property interest.

Prior to the Technical and Miscellaneous Revenue Act of 1988 (TAMRA), it was generally believed that the irrevocable election of a joint and survivor annuity would not qualify for the marital deduction. The survivor annuity was thought to be a nondeductible terminable interest because the participant might possess or enjoy the property after the failure of the

---

[320] TRA 86 § 1852(e)(2)(A), repealing Code § 2517.
[321] Code § 408(e)(4).
[322] Code § 2503(f).

interest transferred to the donee spouse if the donee spouse died first. In addition, there were a number of private letter rulings issued by the IRS dealing with Civil Service benefits that held that the irrevocable election constituted a taxable gift and did not qualify for the marital deduction. Despite these rulings and the possible application of the nondeductible terminal interest rule, it might have been argued that because a joint and survivor annuity is mandated under REA, the failure to elect out of the joint and survivor annuity should not be treated as a taxable gift.[323] There is no authority on this question, since qualifying for the marital deduction has only been a concern since TRA 86's repeal of the gift tax exclusion for transfers of qualified retirement plan benefits and IRAs.

Fortunately, TAMRA provided that an interest in a joint and survivor annuity transferred to a spouse in which only the spouses have any right to receive payments before the death of a surviving spouse automatically qualifies for the marital deduction as QTIP property, unless the donor participant irrevocably elects out of QTIP property treatment.[324]

If automatic QTIP treatment applies, and the donee spouse dies before the participant, no amount is includible in the gross estate of the donee spouse,[325] although under normal QTIP rules, the value of the entire QTIP must be includible in the donee spouse's estate when he or she dies. In a community property state, the nonparticipant spouse who predeceases the participant spouse will not have a community property interest in a qualified retirement plan benefit, since that interest will have been preempted by federal law. Therefore, there should be no interest to include in the nonparticipant spouse's estate.[326] However, many commentators believe that federal law preemption of state community property laws will not extend to amounts that were rolled over from a qualified retirement plan to an IRA prior to the nonparticipant spouse's death. As will be discussed, the nonparticipant spouse's community property interest in the IRA may not qualify for the marital deduction even if the surviving participant spouse is the primary beneficiary, although TRA 97 has clarified the treatment in some cases.[327]

---

[323] *Harris v. Commissioner,* 340 U.S. 106 (1950), holding that a transfer decreed by a court was not a gift.

[324] TAMRA § 6152(b), which added Code § 2523(f)(6).

[325] Code § 2523(f)(6)(D).

[326] *Boggs v. Boggs*, 520 U.S. 833 (1997).

[327] See TRA 97 § 1311(a), amending Code § 2056(b)(7).

Another exception to the normal QTIP rules permits the participant to transfer his or her interest in the benefit without having the donee spouse's interest treated as being transferred as well.[328] The transfer will be treated as a transfer of only the participant's interest, not the entire value of the benefit. Under normal QTIP rules, a transfer of any interest in the QTIP is deemed to be a taxable gift by the donee spouse of the entire value of the QTIP.

B. Estate Taxation

1. *Includibility and Transition Rules*

Prior to 1982, the value of qualified retirement plan benefits and IRAs was excludible from the federal gross estate if ten-year averaging was not elected and the benefits were not payable directly or indirectly to the estate. TEFRA reduced the exclusion to $100,000 for decedents dying after December 31, 1982,[329] and the Deficit Reduction Act of 1984 (DEFRA) repealed the $100,000 exclusion for participants dying after December 31, 1984.[330] Consequently, the value of qualified retirement plan benefits and IRAs payable to the participant's estate or to his or her beneficiaries at his or her death is included in the participant's gross estate for federal estate tax purposes.[331]

However, two important transition rules continue to have validity: one dealing with the unlimited exclusion and the other with the $100,000 exclusion. Although these transition rules were contained in the legislation that reduced and eventually eliminated the exclusion, the transition rules were substantially modified by TRA 86. Under the modified transition rule, the unlimited exclusion is available to the estate of a participant who separated from service before January 1, 1983, as long as the participant has not changed the form of benefit before his or her death. The exclusion applies even if the benefits are not payable pursuant to an irrevocable election and the participant was not receiving benefits as of January 1, 1983.[332] In addition, the $100,000 exclusion is available to the estate of a participant who separated from service before January 1, 1985, as long as the participant has not changed the form of benefit before his or her death.

---

[328] Code § 2523(f)(6)(C).
[329] TEFRA § 245(a).
[330] DEFRA § 525(a).
[331] Code § 2039(a).
[332] TRA 86 § 1852(e)(3).

The $100,000 exclusion applies even if the benefits are not payable pursuant to an irrevocable election and the participant was not receiving benefits as of January 1, 1985.[333] The IRS has ruled that the liberalized transition rule does not apply to IRAs, based on the Conference Committee Report and the fact that separation from service has no relevance to an IRA.[334]

The transition rules will apply only to the extent that the benefits are not directly or indirectly paid to the estate and only if ten-year averaging is not elected. The executor or personal representative of an estate entitled to one of the exclusions must choose between special income tax treatment and one of the exclusions. To make the choice, an irrevocable election must be made on Form 706. If a return including the benefit in the gross estate has already been filed, a request for refund must be filed.[335]

As a result of these transition rules, the estate advisor must ascertain whether a participant or a deceased participant's estate qualifies for one of the transition rules allowing either the unlimited exclusion or the $100,000 exclusion. A retired participant who separated from service before 1983, in the case of the unlimited exclusion, or before 1985, in the case of the $100,000 exclusion, and who desires to change the form of benefit should consider the estate tax consequences if the transition rule becomes unavailable because of the change. In addition, the personal representative of the estate of a participant who separated from service before the relevant date should take advantage of the exclusion if available and if it is appropriate under the circumstances not to elect special averaging.

2. *Qualifying for the Marital Deduction*

A married participant's qualified retirement plan benefits and IRAs should usually be payable in a manner that will qualify the benefits and IRAs for the marital deduction if the participant's federal gross estate is likely to exceed the applicable exclusion amount ($5,430,000 in 2015) and the participant has sufficient assets outside of the qualified retirement plan benefits and IRAs to fund a credit shelter bequest or has decided to rely on portability to use his or her applicable exclusion amount. On the other hand, if the participant does not have sufficient assets outside of qualified

---

[333] *Id.*

[334] Rev. Rul. 92-22, 1992-1 C.B. 313; TAM 9144046.

[335] Treas. Reg. § 20.2039-4(d).

retirement plan benefits and IRAs to fund fully the credit shelter bequest, it may be desirable to use some or all of the benefits or IRAs for this purpose.

Because it is not necessary to use the marital deduction in order to avoid tax on the value of assets equal to the applicable exclusion amount, it was common for a married couple with a combined estate that exceeds that amount, at the death of the first spouse to die, to transfer an amount equal to the applicable exclusion amount to a trust for the benefit of the surviving spouse or to other beneficiaries. The trust, often referred to as a *bypass trust* or *credit shelter trust*, was designed to keep the assets out of the surviving spouse's estate while giving the surviving spouse the enjoyment of the income. As the result of enactment portability beginning in 2011, which allows the surviving spouse to use the unused applicable exclusion amount of the first spouse to die by filing an estate tax return whether it is otherwise required, the use of a credit shelter trust is no longer necessary to avoid wasting the applicable exclusion of the first spouse to die. There may be other reasons for using a credit shelter trust rather than depending on portability, but that is outside the scope of this monograph.

If the benefits and IRAs are not being paid outright to the participant's surviving spouse, additional requirements must often be satisfied to qualify the benefits or IRAs for the marital deduction.

An outright distribution from a qualified retirement plan or IRA directly to a spouse who is a United States citizen qualifies for the marital deduction whether or not the spouse decides to use a spousal rollover. As discussed in Section H of Chapter Three, a surviving spouse may roll over a distribution of the deceased spouse's qualified retirement plan benefit or IRA into his or her own IRA (or, after 2001, a qualified retirement plan).[336] A surviving spouse also may treat a deceased spouse's IRA as his or her own.[337]

If the surviving spouse has the right to withdraw the entire balance of the deceased spouse's accrued benefit, the accrued benefit qualifies for the marital deduction even if the surviving spouse leaves the accrued benefit

---

[336] Code § 402(c)(9).

[337] Treas. Reg. § 1.408-8, A-5(a).

in the plan.[338] Since the spouse has the right to withdraw all of the income and all of the principal at any time, the requirements are satisfied for the life estate/general power of appointment exception to the nondeductible terminable interest rule. Because there is no constructive receipt for income tax purposes with respect to amounts held in a qualified retirement plan or IRA, the spouse will not be taxed on any of the amount held in the plan or IRA until he or she actually receives a distribution. If the benefits are left in the plan, the minimum distribution rules discussed in Section C of Chapter Two must be satisfied.

Prior to TAMRA, it was widely held that a survivor annuity payable to the nonparticipant spouse should qualify for the marital deduction. Because no one else had the right to receive the property upon the death of the surviving spouse, it was not a nondeductible terminable interest. TAMRA clarified this point by requiring automatic QTIP treatment for a survivor annuity unless the executor elects out of QTIP treatment.[339] This provision generally is effective for decedents dying after December 31, 1981.[340]

It is unclear whether automatic QTIP treatment applies to payments made in a form other than a straight life annuity. For example, automatic QTIP treatment may not apply to periodic payments over a period certain equal to the life expectancy of the decedent's spouse, since this form of payment is not a straight annuity and payments may be made to someone other than the spouse if the spouse dies before the specified number of payments have been made. However, if automatic QTIP treatment does not apply to the right to receive installments over a period certain, the rule seems to have been unnecessary, since a straight annuity payable to the spouse is not a nondeductible terminable interest because no one else will receive any payments from the annuity.

A lump sum distribution to a trust will qualify for the marital deduction if the trust itself qualifies for the marital deduction as a life estate/general power of appointment trust, a QTIP trust, an estate trust, or a charitable remainder trust having the surviving spouse as the only noncharitable beneficiary.

---

[338] Rev. Rul. 82-184, 1982-2 C.B. 215; Treas. Reg. § 20.2056(b)-5(f)(6).
[339] TAMRA § 6152(a), adding Code § 2056(b)(7)(C).
[340] TAMRA § 6152(c)(1).

The assets attributable to the participant's benefit may be retained in the trust of the qualified retirement plan under a subtrust that qualifies for the marital deduction as a life estate/general power of appointment trust, a QTIP trust, an estate trust, or charitable remainder trust.[341] Payments from such a trust must also satisfy the minimum distribution rules.

A QTIP trust may be named as the beneficiary of a plan benefit or IRA. A QTIP trust must distribute the income from the assets held in the trust to the surviving spouse at least annually.[342] The regulations interpreting this requirement in connection with a life income/general power of appointment trust require that either the assets in the trust be income producing or the surviving spouse have the right to demand that the trustee convert unproductive assets to productive assets or distribute other assets equal in value to the income that would have been produced by the unproductive assets if they were productive assets.[343] The requirement is also satisfied even if the income is retained in the trust, as long as the spouse has a continuing and unrestricted right to demand that the income be distributed to him or her at any time.[344] The final QTIP regulations adopt these rules for purposes of determining whether the spouse is entitled to all the income at least annually.[345]

If the income generated by the decedent's plan benefits or IRAs is not currently distributed to the QTIP trust and then redistributed to the surviving spouse, the IRS could take the position that the income requirement has not been satisfied. However, if the trustee of the QTIP trust has the right to withdraw the plan benefit or IRA at any time, as is the typical case, and the surviving spouse has the right to require the trustee to make unproductive assets productive, there should be no requirement that any amount be paid out to the QTIP trust from the plan or IRA until required under the minimum distribution rules. Note that because the constructive receipt doctrine does not apply to qualified retirement plan benefits and IRAs, the trust will not be taxable on amounts subject to the trustee's right to withdraw that are not actually withdrawn.

The income generated by the plan benefit or IRA will exceed the amount required to be distributed to the QTIP trust under the minimum

---

[341] Priv. Ltr. Rul. 8843033.
[342] Code § 2056(b)(7)(B)(ii)(1).
[343] Treas. Reg. §§ 20.2056(b)-5(f)(4), (5).
[344] Treas. Reg. § 20.2056(b)-5(f)(8).
[345] Treas. Reg. § 20.2056(b)-7(d)(2).

distribution rules in two situations. If the participant dies before the participant reaches age 70½ and the surviving spouse is the sole designated beneficiary, payments do not have to commence to the trust until the participant would have reached age 70½.[346] The surviving spouse will be treated as the sole beneficiary if all distributions that are made to the trust during the spouse's lifetime are required to be paid out to the spouse.[347]

Once the payments begin, the required distribution in the first few years may not equal the income generated by the plan benefit or IRA. For example, if the surviving spouse is age 59 when the participant would have reached age 70½, the spouse's life expectancy will be 26.1 years. Consequently, the first required minimum distribution will be less than 4 percent of the value of the plan benefits and IRAs, which may be considerably below the income they generate during the year.

Initially the IRS, in one published ruling and a number of private letter rulings, had led commentators to conclude that the plan benefit or IRA itself must satisfy the requirements of a QTIP trust and that the executor of the deceased participant's estate must make the QTIP election with respect to the plan benefit or IRA.[348] Under this view, in order for the plan benefit or IRA to satisfy the QTIP requirements, the form of payment of the plan benefit or IRA selected by the participant before his or her death had to require that an amount at least equal to the income generated by the plan benefit or IRA be payable to the QTIP trust. Furthermore, under the terms of the QTIP trust, income distributions from the plan or IRA had to be treated as income for trust accounting purposes so that it would be redistributed to the spouse. Satisfying the IRS's position required an earlier or larger distribution from the plan or IRA than would have been required under the minimum distribution rules, thereby accelerating the payment of income tax on the benefit or IRA.

Fortunately, in Revenue Ruling 2000-2,[349] the IRS ruled that an IRA payable to a QTIP trust would qualify for the marital deduction as long as the surviving spouse had the right to compel the trustee of the QTIP trust to withdraw the income earned on the assets held by the IRA during the

---

[346] Code § 401(a)(9)(B)(iv).

[347] Treas. Reg. § 1.401(a)(9)-5, A-7(c)(3), *Examples 1 and 2.*

[348] Rev. Rul. 89-89, 1989-2 C.B. 231; Priv. Ltr. Ruls. 9416016, 9321059, 9245033, 9220007.

[349] 2000-3 I.R.B. 305.

year and distribute that amount from the trust to the spouse. The ruling does not deal with the potential gift tax consequences that may arise if the spouse does not exercise his or her right to compel the trustee to withdraw and distribute the income from the IRA to him or her. The failure to demand distribution of the income could be treated as a gift to the remainder beneficiaries to the extent the right was not cumulative; that is, the right only applied to the income earned during the current year and after the end of the year, the power to withdraw the income for that year lapses. The amount of the deemed gift would only include the amount of income during the year in excess of $5,000 or 5 percent of the trust assets.[350] The deemed gift could result in the spouse being treated as making a gift of the entire value of the trust assets under Code § 2519, which treats any gift of an interest in a QTIP trust as a gift of the entire trust.

No gift would occur if the spouse's right was cumulative; that is, the spouse could demand the distribution not only of the current year's income, but all accumulated income as well. At the spouse's death, to the extent the spouse had not exercised his or her right to demand distribution of the income, the accumulated income would be includible in his or her estate because he or she would have a general power of appointment under Code § 2041. Although the assets in the QTIP trust would be includible in the spouse's estate under Code § 2044 if the QTIP election had been made, the inclusion under Code § 2041 would eliminate any benefit of making a partial QTIP election to have some estate tax paid when the first spouse died, since all the trust assets attributable to the accumulated income would still be includible in the surviving spouse's estate because of the power of appointment even though no or a partial QTIP election was made. In addition, because the spouse would become the transferor of the assets over which he or she had a general power of appointment, the reverse QTIP election under Code § 2652(a)(3) may not apply to those assets. The trust agreement could provide that the portion of the trust for which the QTIP election is not made will be held in a separate trust over which the surviving spouse would not have a general power of appointment.[351]

---

[350] Code § 2514(e).

[351] *Estate of Clayton v. Commissioner*, 976 F.2d 1486 (5th Cir. 1992); Treas. Reg. § 20.2056(b)-7(d)(3)(i), allowing an alternate disposition of the part of the trust for which the QTIP election is not made.

A completed gift could also be avoided if the spouse had a special power of appointment with respect to the amount he or she could have withdrawn, but the same issues with respect to a partial or a reverse QTIP election would arise, since the assets subject to the power of appointment would be includible under Code § 2036(a)(1), because the spouse would be entitled to the income from those assets for his or her lifetime, and under Code § 2038, because the spouse retained the right to alter or amend the transfer. The portion of the trust for which the QTIP election is not made could be excluded from the surviving spouse's estate by limiting the spouse's right to demand distributions of income from the plan or IRA and the corresponding general or special power of appointment to the portion of the plan benefit or IRA for which the QTIP election was made.

It would be hoped that the IRS would take the position that the spouse's failure to exercise his or her right was not a transfer subject to gift tax, on the same theory that the failure of a surviving spouse to elect to take his or her statutory share under state law of the deceased's spouse's estate has not been treated as a taxable transfer and because the trust assets remaining at the spouse's death will be subject to transfer tax unless they were taxed at the death of the first spouse because no or a partial QTIP election was made. The same issue has always been present when a trust designed to qualify for the marital deduction, whether as a life income/general power of appointment trust or a QTIP trust, contained unproductive assets and the spouse had a right to compel the trustee to convert the unproductive assets to productive assets.

Revenue Ruling 2000-2 was subsequently modified and superseded by Rev. Rul. 2006-26.[352] In Rev. Rul. 2006-26, the IRS included three state law situations concerning QTIPs, IRAs, and the determination of income under a state's Principal and Income Act or Unitrust Statute.

In Situation 1, the trust is governed by state law that allows the trustee to make adjustments between income and principal to fulfill the trustee's duty of impartiality between the income and remainder beneficiaries, with special provisions applicable to IRAs. Each year, the trustee determines the total return of the trust assets, exclusive of the IRA, and then determines the respective portion of the total return allocated to income and principal. The trustee distributes the amount allocated to income to the

[352] 2006-22 I.R.B. 939.

surviving spouse (S). The trustee makes a similar analysis for the IRA's total return and, if S exercises her withdrawal power, distributes the income portion to her.

In Situation 2, the trust is governed by state law allowing trust income to be a unitrust amount of 4 percent of the fair market value of the trust's assets valued annually. The trustee determines 4 percent of the trust's assets, exclusive of the IRA, and distributes that amount to S each year. The trustee makes a similar determination for the IRA and, if S exercises her withdrawal power, distributes that amount to S.

In Situation 3, the trust is governed by state law using a traditional definition of income. In determining the amount of income S can withdraw from the IRA each year, the trustee applies state law allocation rules without the power to allocate between income and principal. As in Situations 1 and 2, the trustee determines trust income separately from IRA income.

In Rev. Rul. 2006-26, the IRS ruled that, under the circumstances described in Situations 1, 2, and 3, a surviving spouse will be considered to have a qualifying income interest for life for § 2056(b)(7) QTIP purposes in the IRA (or some other defined contribution qualified retirement plan described in § 4974(c)) and in the trust. The IRS clarified that the trust's income and the IRA's income are determined separately in each case and without taking into account the IRA distribution made to the trust. If a marital deduction is desired, the IRS continues to require that the QTIP election be made for both the IRA and the trust.

The IRS stated that the results in Situations 1, 2, and 3 would be the same in each case if the trust directed the trustee annually to withdraw all IRA income and distribute at least the IRA income to S (rather than giving S the power to compel the trustee to do so each year). The IRS noted that S will not be the sole designated beneficiary of the decedent's IRA in situations in which any portion of any distribution from the IRA to the trust may be held in the trust for future distribution (rather than being distributed to S currently). Thus, in such cases, the IRS continues to require that both S and the remainder beneficiaries must be taken into account as designated beneficiaries for IRA distribution purposes.

If someone other than the spouse is entitled to receive payments after the death of the spouse and automatic QTIP treatment does not apply, the interest still may qualify for the marital deduction under the QTIP rules. The Technical Corrections Act of 1982[353] amended the QTIP rules to permit an annuity to be treated as an income interest in property (regardless of whether the property from which the annuity is payable can be separately identified) to the extent provided in regulations.[354]

Under proposed regulations, the value of the deductible interest was determined by comparing the annual annuity payment with a hypothetical yield on the value of the benefit using the current interest rate under Code § 2031 (which is 120 percent of the federal mid-term rate).[355] If the amount of the annual annuity payment was equal to or greater than a yield equal to 120 percent of the mid-term federal rate, the entire value of the benefit was deductible. If the amount of the annual annuity payment was less than a yield equal to 120 percent of the mid-term federal rate, the marital deduction was equal to the portion of the benefit that would produce such yield, but less than the value of the entire benefit.

For example, assume that the value of a deceased participant's interest in the plan is $500,000, the surviving spouse is the sole beneficiary while he or she is alive, and the annual amount to be paid to the spouse is $20,000. Assuming an interest rate of 10 percent, the participant's estate would be entitled to a marital deduction of $200,000 (since 10 percent of $200,000 is $20,000). If the annual amount was $60,000 instead, the marital deduction would be allowed for the entire value of the benefit, but not the larger amount ($600,000) that would be required to produce an annual payment of $60,000, again assuming a 10 percent interest rate.

Unfortunately, § 1941 of the Energy Policy Act of 1992[356] amended Code § 2056(b) and Code § 2523(e) and (f) to limit the term *specific portion* to mean a portion determined only on a fractional or percentage basis. When final regulations concerning qualified terminable interest property and other marital deduction issues were issued on February 28, 1994, the preamble indicated that the IRS recognized that some aspects of the 1992 legislation should be the subject of separate proposed regulations under Code § 2056(b)(7). The IRS specifically invited comments on the application of the Energy Policy Act of 1992 to the treatment of annuities

[353] Pub. L. No. 97-448, 96 Stat. 2365.

[354] Code § 2056(b)(7)(B)(ii), flush language.

[355] Prop. Reg. §§ 20.2056(b)-7(c)(2), (e), *Examples 12 and 13*; Code § 7520, added by TAMRA § 5031(a).

[356] Energy Policy Act of 1992, Pub. L. No. 102-486, 106 Stat. 2776.

as described in the last sentence of Code § 2056(b)(7)(B)(ii). Consequently, it is not clear now whether an annuity payable out of a fund that does not qualify for the automatic QTIP election will nonetheless qualify if an election is made. Under a transitional rule, the final regulations permit a right to an annuity to qualify as originally permitted under the proposed regulations for a person dying on or before October 24, 1992.[357]

No marital deduction is allowed if the surviving spouse is not a United States citizen (effective for decedents dying after November 10, 1988), except for property passing to a qualified domestic trust (QDOT).[358] A QDOT requires that at least one trustee of the trust be either a citizen of the United States or a domestic corporation; no principal distributions other than for hardship may be made without the approval of a trustee who is either a U.S. citizen or a domestic corporation; the executor or personal representative must elect QDOT treatment; and the trust must satisfy any other requirements specified in regulations.[359] The Revenue Reconciliation Act of 1989 (RRA 89) authorized the Treasury to issue regulations that would qualify annuities (including qualified retirement plans and IRAs) as QDOTs.[360]

Final regulations dealing with QDOTs were adopted on August 21, 1995. Treasury Regulation § 20.2056A-4(c) provides that an nonassignable annuity or other payment, which includes a qualified retirement plan (an IRA is considered to be nonassignable), will be treated as passing in the form of a QDOT if the surviving spouse agrees either to pay the deferred estate tax on the corpus portion of each distribution or to transfer the corpus portion to a QDOT.

If a qualified retirement plan or IRA is treated as a QDOT, the minimum distribution rules will eventually require principal distributions from the plan or IRA. These principal distributions, under the QDOT rules, will be subject to estate tax, payable presumably by the plan or IRA, as if included in the deceased participant's estate unless paid into another trust qualifying as a QDOT.[361] Although the estate tax may be avoided by distributing the portion of the distribution deemed to be principal to another QDOT, such a bifurcation of the payment may run afoul of the

---

[357] Treas. Reg. § 20.2056(b)-7(e).
[358] Code § 2056(d), added by TAMRA § 5033(a)(1).
[359] Code § 2056A(a).
[360] RRA 89 § 7815(d)(13), adding Code § 2056A(e).
[361] Code § 2056A(b).

minimum distribution rules dealing with the designated beneficiary. These rules require that the designated beneficiary must be the person entitled to the benefits after the participant's death. The estate tax on principal distributions may discourage the executor from electing QDOT treatment for a qualified retirement plan benefit or IRA.

3. *Other Estate Tax Considerations*

If there may not be sufficient assets in the estate outside of qualified retirement plan benefits or IRAs to fund a credit shelter trust and using portability is not desired, consideration should be given to having some or all of the plan benefits and IRAs paid to the credit shelter trust instead of to the spouse or a marital deduction trust. If the surviving spouse or marital trust is named as the primary beneficiary and at the participant's death the credit shelter trust or bequest is underfunded, the surviving spouse or trustee of the marital deduction trust may disclaim some or all of the benefits so that they pass to the credit shelter trust or bequest. If a surviving spouse disclaims a portion of the benefit, the spouse may roll over the remaining portion to his or her own IRA.[362]

Planning for the use of disclaimers should occur before the participant dies. If the spouse is named as the primary beneficiary, the marital deduction trust or credit shelter trust should be named as an alternate beneficiary. In many estate plans, the proper alternate beneficiary will be the trust set up during the participant's lifetime or in the participant's will, which usually will contain a formula designed to divide the trust assets between the marital deduction trust and credit shelter trust to take maximum advantage of the credit amount. In most cases the oldest beneficiary of both trusts will be the same person, the participant's spouse. Another approach is to have the benefits payable to the credit shelter trust, with a provision that if the benefits are disclaimed by the trustee of that trust, the benefits are then payable to a marital deduction trust and, if disclaimed by the trustee of the marital deduction trust, the benefits are then payable outright to the spouse.

In a General Counsel Memorandum, the Chief Counsel's Office recommended that a disclaimer of qualified retirement plan benefits that satisfied the requirements of § 2518(b) and state law was neither a prohibited assignment or alienation under § 401(a)(13) or ERISA § 206(d),

[362] Priv. Ltr. Rul. 9630034.

nor an assignment of income.[363] Identical treatment was accorded IRAs under § 408(b).[364]

The Seventh Circuit Court of Appeals held that a divorce decree whereby a former spouse waived any interest in the other spouse's pension plan was effective to eliminate the former spouse's right to the benefit. The nonalienation rule did not apply because it was not the participant who gave up an interest in the plan.[365] In several private letter rulings,[366] the IRS ruled that a surviving spouse could make a § 2518 qualified disclaimer of an interest in an IRA, and in one ruling,[367] the IRS ruled that a surviving spouse's § 2518 partial disclaimer of an interest in one of her late husband's two IRAs was valid and that a trustee-to-trustee transfer of the nondisclaimed IRA amounts into a new IRA on her own behalf with her children designated as beneficiaries qualified as a § 408(d)(3)(A) tax-free transfer. The IRS has also ruled that a surviving spouse could make a qualified disclaimer under § 2518 of an interest in a money purchase pension plan[368] and that benefits under a profit-sharing plan could be disclaimed under § 2518.[369]

Finally, the preamble to the 2001 proposed regulations dealing with the required minimum distribution rules under § 401(a)(9) and Reg. § 1.401(a)(9)-4, Q&A 4(a), sanctioned the use of a disclaimer for purposes of determining the designated beneficiary.

---

[363] GCM 39858 (9/9/91).

[364] *See, e.g.,* Priv. Ltr. Ruls. 200444033-034 (beneficiary of IRA disclaimed her interest pursuant to irrevocable disclaimer meeting requirements of § 2518; decedent's IRA, payable to trust, can be subdivided by trustee-to-trustee transfers to create two separate IRAs in name of decedent for the benefit of her two nieces; neither Code nor 2002 final regulations preclude posthumous division of IRAs into more than one IRA). However, no opinion was expressed as to whether a transfer of plan benefits that was not a qualified disclaimer under § 2518(b), including a transfer treated as a qualified disclaimer under § 2518(c)(3), would be a prohibited assignment or alienation and whether a transfer of plan benefits intended to qualify as a disclaimer under state law but that failed to qualify as such would be a prohibited assignment or alienation.

[365] *Fox Valley & Vicinity Constr. Workers Pension Fund v. Brown*, 897 F.2d 275(7th Cir. 1990), *cert. denied*, 498 U.S. 820(1990).

[366] Priv. Ltr. Ruls. 9710034, 9551015, 9537005, and 9037048.

[367] Priv. Ltr. Rul. 9723028.

[368] Priv. Ltr. Rul. 9016026.

[369] Priv. Ltr. Rul. 8838075.

In Rev. Rul. 2005-36,[370] the IRS addressed the issue of an IRA beneficiary receiving a required minimum distribution prior to the execution of the disclaimer. The IRS ruled that: (1) a beneficiary's disclaimer of a beneficial interest in a decedent's IRA is a qualified disclaimer under § 2518 (if all of the requirements of that section are met), even though, prior to making the disclaimer, the beneficiary receives the required minimum distribution for the year of the decedent's death from the IRA; (2) the beneficiary may make a qualified disclaimer under § 2518 with respect to all or a portion of the balance of the account, other than the income attributable to the required minimum distribution that the beneficiary received, provided that at the time the disclaimer is made, the disclaimed amount and the income attributable to the disclaimed amount are paid to the beneficiary entitled to receive the disclaimed amount, or are segregated in a separate account; and (3) a person disclaiming his or her entire remaining interest in an IRA will not be considered a designated beneficiary of the IRA for purposes of § 401(a)(9), if the qualified disclaimer is made on or before September 30th of the calendar year following the calendar year of the employee's death, the beneficiary determination date, and if, on or before that September 30th, the disclaimant is paid the income attributable to the required minimum distribution amount, so that the disclaimant is not entitled to any further benefit in the IRA after September 30th of the calendar year following the calendar year of the employee's death.

If a qualified disclaimer is going to be made, it is important to determine when the nine-month period begins to run. If the participant dies before his or her annuity starting date, the nine-month rule should begin to run as of the date of the participant's death, since this is the date the gift of the beneficiary's interest becomes complete. If the participant dies after his or her annuity starting date, the IRS may take the position that the period begins to run on the participant's annuity starting date. Although there are rulings under the Civil Service Retirement Act in which the IRS has taken the position that there is a completed gift as of the annuity starting date,[371] under Code § 2518, the nine-month period should only begin to run on the date the gift becomes complete,[372] which should be the date of death, since the participant should be free to change the beneficiary at any time before his or her death.

---

[370] 2005-26 I.R.B. 1368.

[371] Priv. Ltr. Ruls. 8715010, 8703016, and 8721013.

[372] *See* Treas. Reg. § 25.2518-2(c)(3).

Because qualified retirement plan benefits, traditional IRAs and the earnings portion of Roth IRAs that do not meet the five-year holding period are treated as IRD, they should not be used to satisfy pecuniary bequests, including a pecuniary bequest under a marital deduction formula. Otherwise, the estate will recognize current income equal to the present value of those benefits when the right to receive the benefits is transferred to the beneficiary in satisfaction of the bequest.[373] The use of a fractional share or designating a spouse or trust as beneficiary avoids the immediate recognition of income.[374] However, some commentators believe that gain should not be recognized until the plan benefit or IRA is actually received, citing Code §§ 402(a)(1), 408(d)(l), and 408A(d)(l). A Chief Counsel Advice has taken the position that the satisfaction of a pecuniary bequest to a charitable organization with an interest in an IRA results in current recognition of income and no offsetting charitable deduction.[375]

Since qualified retirement plan benefits, traditional IRAs, and the earnings portion of Roth IRAs that do not meet the five-year holding period are subject to income tax when received, there is an additional reason to name the surviving spouse or marital deduction trust as the beneficiary. Because the assets of the surviving spouse (including the assets remaining in any marital deduction trust) at the spouse's death will be subject to estate tax to the extent they exceed the deceased spouse's unused applicable exclusion amount, the payment of income tax by the spouse or the marital deduction trust will reduce the assets subject to estate tax. If the benefits are paid to the credit shelter trust or younger-generation beneficiaries instead, the payment of income tax will come from assets that will not be subject to estate tax at the death of the surviving spouse.

Likewise, if a participant is charitably inclined, he or she should consider naming a charity as a beneficiary of qualified retirement plan benefits or traditional IRAs. The plan benefits or IRAs will be deductible as charitable bequests and the charity will not be subject to income tax when the benefits are received. The benefits should not be used to fund a pecuniary charitable bequest, to avoid immediate recognition of income to the estate. However, as noted earlier, some commentators believe that income should not be recognized when a plan benefit or IRA is used to

---

[373] Code § 691(a)(2); Treas. Reg. § 1.661(a)-2(f)(1).

[374] Treas. Reg. § 1.691(a)-4(b); Rev. Rul. 55-117, 1955-1 C.B. 233.

[375] CCA 200644020.

satisfy a pecuniary bequest because a recipient only includes the benefit or IRA in gross income when it is actually received.[376]

If only part of the benefits from a qualified retirement plan or traditional IRA are to be paid to a charity, a separate account or separate share should be established at the beneficiary determination date, since a charity cannot be a designated beneficiary. If a separate account or separate share is not established for the charity's portion of the benefit by the beneficiary determination date (September 30 of the calendar year following the calendar year of the participant's death), the participant will be treated as not having a designated beneficiary.[377]

The Pension Protection Act of 2006 included a provision long sought by charitable organizations that enable an individual, under limited circumstances, to make a "qualified charitable distribution." Under the PPA, up to $100,000 of an otherwise taxable distribution from either a traditional or Roth IRA could have been excluded from income in 2006 and 2007 (regardless of whether the distribution occurred before or after the date of enactment), if the distribution was made to a charitable organization other than a private non-operating foundation, supporting organization, or donor-advised fund. There was no deduction for the amount of the distribution, but it was not treated as a charitable deduction for the annual limitation on charitable contributions, which is 50 percent of AGI in the case of cash contributions to a public charity. Subsequent legislation made the exclusion permanent.

If any of the taxpayer's IRAs consisted of nondeductible contributions, the distribution was treated as coming from the portion that would have been includible in income first. Otherwise, the distribution would consist of a pro rata share of the account owner's nondeductible contributions that would not have been included in income in any event. Although a distribution from a Roth IRA qualified as a qualified charitable distribution, there would have been no benefit in using what would already be a tax-free distribution from a Roth IRA to make a charitable contribution. A contribution from any other source would have resulted in an income tax benefit, either as a charitable deduction or as an exclusion from taxable income of an amount that would have otherwise been included in taxable income.

---

[376] Code §§ 402(a), 408(d)(1), 408A(d)(1).
[377] Treas. Reg. § 1.401(a)(9)-5, A-7(a)(2).

The exclusion did not apply if any part of the distribution was not otherwise deductible; for example, where the taxpayer received a benefit from the charity that reduced the amount deductible. In this case, the balance would be includible in gross income but would be eligible as a charitable deduction, subject to the 50 percent AGI limitation. In addition, Notice 2007-7 made it clear that satisfying a charitable pledge would not be treated as self-dealing.

The taxpayer must have been at least 70½ at the time the distribution was made. The distribution satisfied the minimum distribution rules to the extent of the distribution. Notice 2007-7 confirmed that the IRA owner would be treated as having elected out of withholding if the owner designated that the distribution was to be a qualified charitable distribution.

The following taxpayers, assuming they meet all the requirements for a qualified charitable distribution, benefited from this provision:

(1) They wished to make other charitable contributions that would have equaled or exceeded the 50 percent AGI cap;

(2) They wished to avoid the 3 percent haircut on itemized deductions; that is, they had AGI over $309,900 in 2015 for married couples filing joint returns (or $154,950 for married individuals filing separate returns);

(3) They had social security income that would have been taxed (or taxed at a higher rate) if their AGI were increased;

(4) They did not itemize their deductions; or

(5) They lived in states that did not allow charitable deductions in computing taxable income for state tax purposes.

Since qualified retirement plan benefits and IRAs will be includible in the federal gross estate for federal estate tax purposes, the source of payment of the federal estate tax (and state estate and inheritance taxes) should be considered. A state's apportionment statute may not apply to the estate tax on distributions from qualified retirement plans and IRAs. In addition, if the estate taxes are payable by a recipient who is not taking a lump sum distribution, any additional withdrawal from the plan or traditional IRA, or a nonqualified distribution from a Roth IRA, to pay the taxes, will result in additional income tax.

Generally, the testator's desires will be fulfilled if the beneficiaries are required to pay the estate taxes on the benefits they receive. If the spouse is the beneficiary and the marital deduction is desired for the entire amount passing to the spouse, the estate tax should be paid out of other assets.

The generation-skipping transfer (GST) tax, completely revamped by TRA 86, is not discussed in detail in this monograph. In planning for distributions from qualified retirement plans and IRAs, either the GST tax should be avoided altogether or the GST tax exemption ($5,430,000 in 2015) should be allocated to all benefits or IRAs paid to skip persons. Generally speaking, a *skip person* is someone in a generation more than one generation below the participant, such as a grandchild or great-grandchild.

If a participant makes an irrevocable election during his or her lifetime to have some or all of the benefits paid to a skip person after the participant's death, an allocation of any of the participant's GST exemption to the value of the benefit payable to the skip person will not be effective at the time of the election if the benefit will be includible in the participant's federal gross estate.[378] The allocation will not be effective until the earlier of the participant's death or when the benefit will no longer be includible in the participant's estate (*e.g.,* because he or she no longer retains a right to income). In most cases, a qualified retirement plan benefit or IRA will be includible in the participant's estate unless he or she has no right to any portion of the benefit at any time after the irrevocable election is made. Also, an additional allocation of the GST exemption may be required each year if the participant's accrued benefit increases because of continued participation in the plan after the irrevocable election. Irrevocable elections during a participant's lifetime are rare and ordinarily should be avoided, since they can result in immediate gift tax liability and reduce flexibility in future planning.

[378] Code § 2642(f).

Chapter Five

Spousal Rights

A. Survivor Annuities

ERISA gave the participant's spouse only minimal rights in the participant's qualified retirement plan benefits. Under ERISA, the participant was entitled to receive his or her benefit in the form of a joint and survivor annuity unless the participant elected otherwise. However, the participant's spouse was not required to consent to the participant's election not to receive the benefit in the form of a joint and survivor annuity. In addition, a qualified retirement plan was required to provide the participant with the option of having a survivor annuity paid to the participant's surviving spouse if the participant died before he or she had begun to receive benefits. The plan was permitted to charge the participant for this benefit either by requiring the participant to make contributions to pay for the benefit or by reducing the normal retirement benefit payable to the participant and his or her beneficiary.

The Retirement Equity Act of 1984 (REA) now requires all qualified retirement plans to pay part or all of the accrued benefit of a vested participant who dies before his or her annuity starting date to his or her surviving spouse either outright or in the form of a qualified preretirement survivor annuity.[379] In addition, most qualified retirement plans are required to pay the accrued benefit of a vested participant who is alive on his or her annuity starting date in the form of a qualified joint and survivor annuity.[380] In general, the annuity starting date is the first day of the first period for which an amount is paid to the participant as an annuity or in any other form.[381]

A *qualified joint and survivor annuity* is an annuity for the life of the participant with a survivor annuity for the life of a nonparticipant spouse who survives the participant. The amount of the survivor annuity must not be less than 50 percent nor more than 100 percent of the amount of the annuity payable during the joint lives of the participant and the spouse. If the normal form of the benefit under the plan is not a qualified joint and

---

[379] Code § 401(a)(11)(A)(ii).
[380] Code § 401(a)(11)(A)(i).
[381] Treas. Reg. § 1.401(a)-20, Q&A 10(b)(1).

survivor annuity, the annuity payable during the joint lives of the participant and the participant's spouse must be the actuarial equivalent of the normal form of payment.[382]

In the case of a defined benefit plan, a qualified preretirement survivor annuity means a survivor annuity for the life of the surviving spouse of the participant. The amount of the annuity and the date on which the surviving spouse is entitled to begin to receive the annuity depend on whether the participant dies before or after reaching the earliest retirement age under the plan.[383]

The Pension Protection Act requires that a participant must have the right to elect a qualified optional survivor annuity, which is an annuity for the life of the participant with a survivor annuity for the life of the spouse which is equal to the applicable percentage of the amount of the annuity that is: (1) payable during the joint lives of the participant and the spouse; and (2) the actuarial equivalent of a single annuity for the life of the participant. If the survivor annuity provided by the qualified joint and survivor annuity under the plan is less than 75 percent of the annuity payable during the joint lives of the participant and spouse, the applicable percentage is 75 percent. If the survivor annuity provided by the qualified joint and survivor annuity under the plan is greater than or equal to 75 percent of the annuity payable during the joint lives of the participant and spouse, the applicable percentage is 50 percent. Thus, for example, if the survivor annuity provided by the qualified joint and survivor annuity under the plan is 50 percent, the survivor annuity provided under the qualified optional survivor annuity must be 75 percent.

If the participant dies after reaching the earliest retirement age under the plan, the survivor annuity is equal to the survivor annuity that would have been payable to the surviving spouse under a qualified joint and survivor annuity determined as if the participant had retired the day before he or she died and had elected to receive an immediate qualified joint and survivor annuity.[384]

If the participant dies before the earliest retirement age under the plan, the survivor annuity is equal to the survivor annuity that would have been

[382] Code § 417(b).
[383] Code § 417(c)(1).
[384] Code § 417(c)(1)(A)(i).

payable under a qualified joint and survivor annuity if the participant had separated from service on the date of his or her death, survived to the earliest retirement age, retired with an immediate qualified joint and survivor annuity at the earliest retirement age, and died on the day after the day on which he or she would have reached the earliest retirement age.[385] In this case, the annuity payments do not commence until the deceased participant would have reached the earliest retirement age under the plan.[386]

The vested accrued benefit of a participant in a defined benefit plan payable at death may exceed the cost of providing the survivor annuity, particularly if the plan provides a death benefit funded with life insurance. In this case, the participant may designate someone other than the spouse as the beneficiary of the excess portion of the benefit.

In the case of a defined contribution plan, a qualified preretirement survivor annuity means an annuity for the life of the surviving spouse, the actuarial equivalent of which is not less than 50 percent of the nonforfeitable portion of the account balance of the participant at his or her date of death.[387] Consequently, in the case of a defined contribution plan, the participant may designate someone other than the surviving spouse as the beneficiary of the remaining 50 percent of the nonforfeitable portion of his or her account balance without the spouse's consent.

A participant must be given the right to waive the qualified joint and survivor annuity or qualified preretirement survivor annuity. In addition, a participant must be furnished with notices explaining the survivor annuity forms of benefit.[388] However, if the plan fully subsidizes the cost of each annuity, the right to waive the qualified joint and survivor annuity or qualified preretirement survivor annuity and the right to notices explaining the survivor annuity forms do not have to be provided.[389]

A plan fully subsidizes the cost of an annuity if under the plan the participant's failure to waive the annuity does not result in either a decrease in the participant's plan benefits or an increase in required

---

[385] Code § 417(c)(1)(A)(ii).
[386] Code § 417(c)(1)(B).
[387] Code § 417(c)(2).
[388] Code § 417(a)(1). The IRS has issued guidance and sample language forms to satisfy the notice requirement. IRS Notice 97-10, 1997-1 C.B. 370.
[389] Code § 417(a)(5)(A).

contributions from the participant.[390] Under the regulations, a plan that offers a lump sum distribution option does not fully subsidize the cost of a qualified joint and survivor annuity.[391] A qualified preretirement survivor annuity is fully subsidized in a defined contribution plan. Because the value of the annuity in this case is equal to 50 percent of the participant's nonforfeitable benefit, the participant does not incur any loss of benefit or increase in required contributions as a result of the survivor annuity.[392] Even if the plan fully subsidizes the cost of one of the required annuities, spousal consent, as described hereafter, is required if the participant wants to designate someone other than his or her spouse as the beneficiary.[393]

The spouse must consent to the participant's election to waive either the qualified joint and survivor or qualified preretirement survivor annuity.[394] The consent form must be in writing and must designate a beneficiary and a form of benefit, neither of which may be changed without the spouse's consent unless the spouse signs a general consent.[395] Under a general consent, a spouse may expressly permit the participant to change the beneficiary designation or form of payment or both without the spouse's consent.[396] A general consent is only allowed if the plan document specifically authorizes it.[397] Furthermore, a general consent must expressly state that the spouse has the right to limit his or her consent to a specific beneficiary and a specific optional form of benefit and that the spouse voluntarily elects to relinquish both of such rights or, if applicable, either of such rights.[398] The spouse's consent, whether or not a general consent, must acknowledge the effect of the election and must be witnessed by a plan representative or a notary public.[399] If the beneficiary is a revocable trust, the spouse need only consent to the designation of the trust and need not consent to the designation of trust beneficiaries or any changes of trust beneficiaries.[400]

---

[390] Code § 417(a)(5)(B).
[391] Treas. Reg. § 1.401(a)-20, Q&A 38(a)(2), *Example (1).*
[392] Treas. Reg. § 1.401(a)-20, Q&A 38(b).
[393] Code § 417(a)(5)(A).
[394] Code § 417(a)(2)(A)(i).
[395] Treas. Reg. § 1.401(a)-20, Q&A 31(b).
[396] Treas. Reg. § 1.401(a)-20, Q&A 31(c).
[397] Treas. Reg. § 1.401(a)-20, Q&A 31(c).
[398] Treas. Reg. § 1.401(a)-20, Q&A 31(c).
[399] Code § 417(a)(2)(A)(iii).
[400] Treas. Reg. § 1.401 (a)-20, Q&A 31(a).

A waiver of the qualified preretirement survivor annuity does not have to specify the optional form of preretirement benefit. The participant may also change the form of benefit, but not the beneficiary, without the consent of the spouse, unless the spouse has signed a general consent permitting the participant to change the beneficiary without his or her consent.[401] Although the regulations are not free from doubt, a spouse should be able to sign a general consent to a waiver of his or her right to a death benefit under a defined contribution plan that is not subject to the qualified survivor annuity rules. The form of benefit may be changed without the spouse's consent.[402]

A beneficiary designation executed before August 23, 1984, that names someone other than the spouse as the primary beneficiary, whether or not the spouse consented to the designation, is not valid to deprive the spouse of his or her right to a qualified preretirement survivor annuity or to the participant's nonforfeitable accrued benefit under a defined contribution plan not subject to the qualified survivor annuity rules.[403]

A participant's waiver of the qualified joint and survivor annuity or a qualified preretirement survivor annuity and the spouse's consent to the waiver will be valid only if made during specific election periods.[404] The waiver of the qualified joint and survivor annuity may be made only during the 180-day period ending on the first day of the period for which the first payment is to be made (the annuity starting date), and only after a notice explaining the qualified joint and survivor annuity has been distributed to the participant.[405] If the participant defers the commencement of regular distributions, but in the meantime makes withdrawals of some of his or her benefit, the spouse must consent to a waiver of the qualified joint and survivor annuity within the 180-day period ending on the date of each withdrawal.[406]

The statutory language states that the waiver of a qualified preretirement survivor annuity may be made only on or after the first day of the plan year in which the participant attains age 35.[407] Fortunately, the regulations

---

[401] Treas. Reg. § 1.401(a)-20, Q&A 31(b)(2).
[402] Treas. Reg. § 1.401(a)-20, Q&A 32(b).
[403] Treas. Reg. § 1.401(a)-20, Q&A 43.
[404] Code § 417(a)(6).
[405] Code § 417(a)(6)(A).
[406] Treas. Reg. § 1.401(a)-20, Q&A 9, 10(a).
[407] Code § 417(a)(6)(B).

permit a waiver to be made when participation commences if the participant has not yet reached age 35, but require such a participant to execute a new waiver after reaching age 35.[408] Consequently, a participant who wants to waive both the qualified preretirement survivor annuity and the qualified joint and survivor annuity and who begins to participate in a plan before he or she reaches age 35 must obtain the consent of the spouse at least three times: when participation begins, after the participant reaches age 35, and during the 90-day period ending on the date of the participant's annuity starting date.

In a defined contribution plan that is not required to provide the qualified preretirement survivor annuity and qualified joint and survivor annuity, a participant's spouse may waive his or her right to the death benefit (which is the participant's entire nonforfeitable accrued benefit in the plan) at any time after participation commences, regardless of the participant's age.[409]

A participant must be permitted to revoke his or her election to waive the survivor annuities at any time during the applicable election period.[410] However, a plan may require that the spouse's consent to a waiver of the qualified preretirement or joint and survivor annuity not be revocable.[411] A plan may, but is not required to, permit a surviving spouse to change the optional form of benefit payable after the participant's death.[412]

The notice required to be furnished to the participant must explain the terms and conditions of the annuity, the participant's right to make an election to waive the annuity form of benefit and the effect of such an election, the rights of the participant's spouse, and the right to make and the effect of a revocation of an election.[413]

The notice describing the qualified joint and survivor annuity must be furnished no more than 90 days nor less than 30 days before the annuity starting date.[414] However, a plan may actually begin distributions seven

[408] Treas. Reg. § 1.401(a)-20, Q&A 33(b).
[409] Treas. Reg. § 1.401(a)-20, Q&A 33(a).
[410] Code § 417(a)(1)(A)(ii); Treas. Reg. § 1.401(a)-20, Q&A 30.
[411] Treas. Reg. § 1.401(a)-20, Q&A 30.
[412] Treas. Reg. § 1.401(a)-20, Q&A 31(b)(3).
[413] Code § 417(a)(3); Treas. Reg. §§ 1.401(a)-20, Q&A 36, 1.401(a)-11(c)(3).
[414] Code § 417(a)(3)(A); Regs. §§ 1.417(e)-1(b)(3), 1.401(a)-20, Q&A-36; *see also* Regs. § 1.411(a)-11(c)(2). The IRS issued final regulations under § 417(a)(7) permitting required written explanations of certain benefits to be provided by qualified retirement plans after the annuity starting date. T.D. 9076, 68 Fed. Reg. 41906 (7/16/03). *See* Regs.

days after a participant elects a form of distribution and his or her spouse consents to it.[415] The notice describing the qualified preretirement survivor annuity must be provided during whichever of the following periods ends last:[416]

(1) The period beginning with the first day of the plan year in which the participant reaches age 32 and ending with the close of the plan year preceding the plan year in which the participant reaches age 35;

(2) The period beginning one year before and ending one year after the participant becomes a participant in the plan;

(3) The period beginning one year before and ending one year after the qualified preretirement survivor annuity ceases to be fully subsidized;

(4) The period beginning one year before and ending one year after the participant first becomes subject to the qualified survivor annuity rules by electing an annuity form of payment under an otherwise exempt defined contribution plan; and

(5) If the participant separates from service before age 35, the period beginning one year before and ending one year after the separation.

A plan does not have to offer a qualified joint and survivor annuity or qualified preretirement survivor annuity unless the participant and spouse have been married throughout the one-year period ending on the earlier of the participant's annuity starting date or the date of the participant's death.[417] If the participant is married on the annuity starting date, then the benefit must commence to be paid in the form of a qualified joint and survivor annuity, unless the participant, with the spouse's consent, elects otherwise. The plan may provide that the spouse will not be entitled to a survivor benefit if there is a divorce or the participant dies before the end of the one-year period beginning on the day they are married.[418]

---

§ 1.417(e)-1(b)(3). The final regulations were effective July 16, 2003. Preamble, T.D. 9076, 68 Fed. Reg. 41906 (7/16/03).

[415] Treas. Reg. § 1.417(e)-1(b)(3)(ii).

[416] Code § 417(a)(3)(B)(ii); Treas. Reg. § 1.401(a)-20, Q&A 35.

[417] Code § 417(d)(1).

[418] Treas. Reg. § 1.401(a)-20, Q&A 25(b)(2)(i).

If a participant marries within one year before the annuity starting date and the participant and the participant's spouse in such marriage have been married for at least a one-year period ending on or before the date of the participant's death, the participant and the spouse will be treated as having been married throughout the one-year period ending on the participant's annuity starting date and the spouse will be entitled to a survivor annuity determined as if the participant had elected a qualified joint and survivor annuity.[419]

A plan subject to the qualified survivor annuity rules must provide that a spouse must consent to the use of the participant's accrued benefit as a security for a loan from the plan.[420]

A defined contribution plan other than a money purchase pension plan is not required to provide the qualified survivor annuities with respect to a participant under the following conditions:[421]

(1) The plan provides that the participant's nonforfeitable accrued benefit (reduced by any security interest held by the plan by reason of a loan outstanding to the participant) is payable in full to the participant's surviving spouse on the death of the participant (or, if there is no surviving spouse or the surviving spouse consents as described earlier, the benefit is payable to a designated beneficiary);

(2) The participant does not elect to have the benefits paid in the form of a life annuity; and

(3) The plan does not receive, directly or indirectly, assets that will be allocated to the participant's account after December 31, 1984, from a plan that is required to provide the qualified joint and survivor annuity and qualified preretirement survivor annuity. However, if such assets are accounted for separately, only those assets will be subject to the survivor annuity rules.[422]

In addition, an ESOP, which may be in part a money purchase pension plan, is not subject to the qualified survivor annuity rules to the extent a

---

[419] Code § 417(d)(2).
[420] Code § 417(a)(4).
[421] Code § 401(a)(11)(B)(iii); Treas. Reg. § 1.401(a)-20, Q&A 3(a).
[422] Code § 401(a)(11)(B), flush language.

participant has a right to demand a distribution of employer securities.[423] Finally, IRAs, SEPs, and presumably SIMPLE IRA plans are not subject to the spousal consent rules.[424]

Because a qualified retirement plan must pay a surviving spouse either a qualified preretirement survivor annuity or the participant's nonforfeitable accrued benefit if the participant dies before his or her annuity starting date, all or part of the death benefit payable under any type of qualified retirement plan must be paid to the spouse unless he or she consents otherwise.

No consent by the participant or the spouse to a benefit payment is required if:

(1) The present value of the participant's accrued benefit has never exceeded $5,000;[425]

(2) The benefit is paid in the form of a qualified joint and survivor annuity if the benefit is subject to the survivor annuity rules or in the normal form under the plan in other cases and the benefit is paid on or after the date the participant attains the later of age 62 or the normal retirement age under the plan;[426]

(3) The benefit is payable after the death of the participant unless the plan is subject to the qualified survivor annuity rules and the participant's beneficiary is the spouse;[427]

(4) The benefit is payable to an alternate payee under a QDRO unless the QDRO provides otherwise;[428]

(5) The benefit is required to be paid to satisfy the minimum distribution rules under Code § 401(a)(9);[429]

---

[423] Treas. Reg. § 1.401(a)-20, Q&A 3(c).
[424] Treas. Reg. § 1.401(a)-20, Q&A 3(d).
[425] Treas. Reg. § 1.417(e)-l(b)(2)(i). TRA 97 § 1071(a), amending Code §§ 417(e) and 411(a)(11)(A), changed the $3,500 to $5,000 for plan years beginning after August 5, 1997.
[426] Treas. Reg. §§ 1.411(a)-11(c)(4), 1.417(e)-1(b)(1).
[427] Treas. Reg. §§ 1.411(a)-11(c)(5), 1.417(e)-1(b)(1).
[428] Treas. Reg. § 1.411(a)-11(c)(6).
[429] Treas. Reg. § 1.411(a)-11(c)(7).

(6) The benefit is required to be paid to satisfy the benefit limitations of Code § 415;[430]

(7) The benefit consists of dividends on stock held by an ESOP to which the special deduction provisions of Code § 404(k) apply;[431] or

(8) The benefit is payable due to the termination of a defined contribution plan that does not offer an annuity option, but only if the employer (or any member of a controlled group of corporations including the employer) does not maintain another defined contribution plan other than an ESOP.[432] If the employer does maintain another defined contribution plan, the participant's balance in the terminating plan may be transferred to the continuing plan without the participant's consent. Of course, any distribution from a plan must be in accordance with the provisions of the written plan document.

B. Plan Loans

As a general rule, a participant's benefit in a qualified retirement plan may not be assigned or alienated.[433] In addition to the exception for QDROs added by REA in 1984, there are three statutory or regulatory exceptions to this nonalienation rule. The first exception permits a participant who has retired and begun to receive benefits to make a voluntary and revocable assignment of up to 10 percent of any benefit payment unless the assignment is made for the purpose of defraying plan administration costs.[434] Second, the IRS may levy a participant's benefit to pay taxes owed by the participant.[435] Third, a participant may secure a loan from the plan with his or her vested accrued benefit if the loan meets certain requirements so that it is not a prohibited transaction under Code § 4975.[436]

---

[430] Treas. Reg. § 1.411(a)-11(c)(7).
[431] Treas. Reg. § 1.411(a)-11(e)(2).
[432] Treas. Reg. § 1.411(a)-11(e)(1).
[433] Code § 401(a)(13)(A).
[434] *Id.*
[435] Treas. Reg. § 1.401(a)-13(b)(2).
[436] Code § 401(a)(13)(A).

A loan will not be a prohibited transaction if the loan is available to all participants or beneficiaries on a reasonably equivalent basis, is not made available to highly compensated employees in an amount greater than the amount available to other employees, is made in accordance with specific provisions regarding plan loans set forth in the plan, bears a reasonable rate of interest, and is adequately secured.[437] Before 2002, a loan to a sole proprietor, a partner who owned more than10 percent of the capital or profits interest of a partnership, or a shareholder of an S corporation who owned more than 5 percent of the shares was not an exempt loan under this provision.[438] TRA 2001 now permits such loans after 2001.[439]

A loan will be treated as a taxable distribution, subject to ordinary income tax and possibly to the 10 percent penalty on premature distributions unless the following requirements are satisfied.[440] First, the amount of the loan, plus any outstanding loans from the plan, cannot exceed the lesser of (1) $50,000 or (2) the greater of (a) one-half of the present value of the nonforfeitable accrued benefit of the participant under the plan or (b) $10,000. The $50,000 amount is reduced by the excess (if any) of the highest outstanding balance of loans from the plan during the one-year period ending on the day before the day on which the loan is made, over the outstanding balance of loans from the plan on the date on which the loan was made.[441] Consequently, a participant must wait at least one year after paying off a previous loan to borrow the full $50,000 from a plan. All plans of the employer, including related employers under Code § 414(b), (c), and (m), are treated as a single plan for purposes of applying these limitations.[442]

Furthermore, the terms of the loan must require repayment within five years in substantially level payments not less frequently than quarterly.[443] A longer period is permitted if the loan is used to acquire a dwelling unit that the participant intends to use within a reasonable time as his or her principal residence.[444] The loan will also be treated as a taxable

---

437 Code § 4975(d)(1).
438 Former Code § 4975(d), flush language.
439 TRA 2001 § 612, amending Code § 4975(f)(6).
440 Code § 72(p)(1).
441 Code § 72(p)(2).
442 Code § 72(p)(2)(D).
443 Code §§ 72(p)(2)(B)(i), (C).
444 Code § 72(p)(2)(B)(ii).

distribution if it is not paid back within the prescribed period or is extended beyond the prescribed period.

Plan loans are generally not advisable. For one thing, the interest on a loan from a qualified retirement plan is not deductible if the borrower is a key employee or the loan is secured by elective deferrals under a 401(k) plan.[445] In most other cases, interest paid on plan loans will be nondeductible personal interest.

C. Qualified Domestic Relations Orders

Before the enactment of REA, the courts were split as to whether the nonalienation rule preempted state court orders in domestic relations cases.[446] To resolve this conflict, REA created an additional exception to the nonalienation rules for payments made pursuant to a QDRO.[447] Presumably after REA, a qualified retirement plan may not comply with domestic relations orders that do not satisfy the requirements of a QDRO.[448]

A QDRO is a domestic relations order that creates, or recognizes the existence of, an alternate payee's right to receive or assign all or part of the participant's accrued benefit under a qualified retirement plan.[449]

A QDRO may not alter the amount or form of the participant's accrued benefit,[450] and may not require the payment to an alternate payee of benefits that are required to be paid to another alternate payee under another order previously determined to be a QDRO.[451] A domestic relations order must relate to the payment of child support, alimony payments, or marital property rights to an alternate payee[452] and must be made pursuant to a state domestic relations law, including a community

---

[445] Code § 72(p)(3).

[446] *Compare Foster v. Foster,* 589 S.W.2d 223 (Ky. Ct. App. 1979) (holding that plan benefits were marital property, but not discussing preemption), and *In re Marriage of Campa,* 89 Cal. App. 3d 113, 152 Cal. Rptr. 362 (1979), *with Francis v. United Technologies Corp.,* 458 F. Supp. 84 (N.D. Cal. 1978).

[447] Code § 401(a)(13)(B).

[448] Code § 401(a)(13)(B) (by implication).

[449] Code § 414(p)(1)(A)(i).

[450] Code § 414(p)(3)(A).

[451] Code § 414(p)(3)(C).

[452] Code § 414(p)(1)(B)(i).

property law.[453] An *alternate payee* is a spouse, former spouse, child, or other dependent of the participant who is recognized by the domestic relations order as having a right to all or a portion of a participant's accrued benefit.[454]

To qualify as a QDRO, the order must clearly specify the following facts:

(1) The name and last known mailing address (if any) of the participant and the name and mailing address of each alternate payee covered by the order;

(2) The amount or percentage of the participant's benefits to be paid by the plan to each alternate payee, or the manner in which the amount or percentage is to be determined;

(3) The number of payments or period to which the order applies; and

(4) Each plan to which the order applies.[455]

Generally, a QDRO may require that the payment to the alternate payee be made in any form in which the participant's benefits may be paid under the plan.[456] However, a QDRO may not require that the payment be made in the form of a joint and survivor annuity with respect to the alternate payee and his or her subsequent spouse, since payments must be restricted to the former spouse and other alternate payees.

A QDRO may provide that a participant's former spouse is to be treated as the surviving spouse of the participant under the qualified joint and survivor annuity and qualified preretirement survivor annuity rules.[457] In this case, upon the death of the participant the former spouse would be entitled to a survivor annuity, just as if the former spouse were still married to the deceased participant when the participant died.

---

[453] Code § 414(p)(1)(B)(ii).
[454] Code § 414(p)(8).
[455] Code § 414(p)(2). The IRS has issued sample language that may be included in a QDRO. IRS Notice 97-11, 1997-1 C.B. 379.
[456] Code § 414(p)(4)(A)(iii).
[457] Code § 414(p)(5).

Although a QDRO may not require a plan to provide a type or form of benefit or an option not otherwise provided under the plan,[458] a QDRO may require that the payment of benefits be made to the alternate payee before a participant separates from service if the participant has reached the earliest retirement age under the plan.[459] For this purpose, the earliest retirement age is the earlier of (1) the earliest date on which the participant is entitled to a distribution under the plan, regardless of whether he or she separates from service; and (2) the later of the date the participant reaches age 50 or the earliest date on which a participant who separates from service may begin receiving benefits under the plan.[460]

A QDRO may require that the amount of the benefit be determined as if the participant had retired on the date on which the payment is to begin under the QDRO, but taking into account only the present value of the benefits actually accrued at that time.[461] The interest rate assumption used in determining the present value must be the interest rate specified in the plan or, if no interest rate is specified, 5 percent.[462] The lower the interest rate used, the higher the value of the accrued benefit will be. In determining the amount of the benefit, the present value of any employer subsidy for early retirement may be disregarded.[463]

A qualified retirement plan must establish a procedure for determining whether a domestic relations order qualifies as a QDRO.[464] As part of the procedure, the plan administrator must notify the participant and each alternate payee of the receipt of the order and of the plan's procedures for determining whether the order is a QDRO.[465] The plan administrator also must determine within a reasonable period after the receipt of the order whether the order is qualified, and must notify the participant and each alternate payee of the determination.[466]

If the alternate payee is the spouse or former spouse of the participant, the alternate payee is taxed on the amounts received under the QDRO.[467] If

[458] Code § 414(p)(3)(A).
[459] Code § 414(p)(4)(A).
[460] Code § 414(p)(4)(B).
[461] Code § 414(p)(4)(A)(ii).
[462] Code § 414(p)(4), flush language.
[463] Code § 414(p)(4)(A)(ii).
[464] Code § 414(p)(6)(B).
[465] Code § 414(p)(6)(A)(i).
[466] Code § 414(p)(6)(A)(ii).
[467] Code § 402(e)(1)(A).

the alternate payee is not the participant's spouse or former spouse, the participant is taxed on the amount distributed to the alternate payee. However, if the participant is subject to tax on the distribution and does not elect out of withholding, the alternate payee will receive less than the total amount specified in the QDRO.[468]

D. Community Property Law Considerations

1. Introduction

In a community property state, the nonparticipant spouse acquires an interest in the participant's benefits under a qualified retirement plan. The benefit under a qualified retirement plan accrues to the married couple as community property during the marriage and while they live in a community property state.[469] However, as discussed in Subsection 2 of this Section, ERISA preempts enforcement of those community property rights other than with a QDRO. Further, this preemption will continue to apply to a nonparticipant spouse's rights to qualified plan benefits that are distributed from the plan following that spouse's death, including amounts rolled over into an IRA.

While there is some language in the Code indicating that community property laws are to be disregarded in applying the requirements for IRAs, it is generally thought that the nonparticipant spouse is also entitled to a community property interest in the participant's IRA. The Code language was probably designed to allow the participant to use all of his or her compensation for purposes of determining the amount that could be contributed to an IRA each year by the participant and to prevent a nonworking spouse from making IRA contributions based on earnings of the working spouse.[470] Furthermore, since IRAs are, generally, not

---

[468] IRS Notice 89-25, 1989-1 C.B. 662, Q&A 3.

[469] *Bowman v. Bowman,* 217 Cal. Rptr. 174 (4th Dist. 1985); *Estate of Austin,* 206 Cal. App. 3d 1249 (4th Dist. 1988); *Snyder v. Snyder,* 197 Cal. App. 3d 6 (4th Dist. 1987); *Allard v. Frech,* 754 S.W.2d 111 (Tex. 1988); *Farver v. Department of Retirement Sys.,* 644 P.2d 1149 (Wash. 1982); *T. L. James & Co. v. Montgomery,* 332 So. 2d 834 (La. 1975).

[470] *See* Priv. Ltr. Rul. 8040101. In Priv. Ltr. Rul. 199937055, the IRS noted that, according to H.R. Rep. No. 779, 93d Cong., 2d Sess., 1974-3 C.B. 244, 363, community property laws are not to apply with respect to deductions for contributions made to IRAs, and it concluded that this provision clearly applies only to the deduction provisions under Code §§ 219 and 220. Because there is no specific language on the congressional intent of Code § 408(g), and in view of the general rule of statutory construction that federal

covered by ERISA and its broad preemption provisions, community property interests in IRAs are, most likely, subject to enforcement through conventional state probate procedures. However, if state law enforcement mechanisms were preempted regarding benefits in a qualified retirement plan, that preemption continues when the benefit is rolled over into an IRA.

2. *Qualified Retirement Plans*

As discussed in Section C of this chapter, before the enactment of REA, most courts had recognized the rights of a nonparticipant spouse to the participant's plan benefits and IRAs under the domestic relations laws of the various states, including community property laws.[471] In fact, the *Allard* case, decided under Texas law, gave the nonparticipant spouse's estate the right to receive the community property interest of the nonparticipant spouse in a qualified plan.

As a result of REA, since 1984 the nonparticipant spouse has certain rights in qualified retirement plans, which are discussed in detail in Section A of this chapter. REA also established a procedure for a nonparticipant spouse to enforce his or her rights, including community property rights. These rights are enforced through the use of a QDRO, which is discussed in detail in Section C of this chapter.

The QDRO procedure may give a participant and his or her spouse in a harmonious marriage a number of planning opportunities in a community property state that are not available in a common law state—provided that state law allows a QDRO to be issued in this situation. For instance,

---

statutes are construed to avoid preemption of state law unless that was the clear intent of Congress, the IRS reasoned, Code § 408(g) does not abrogate any substantive rights under state law. Therefore, the IRS ruled that the classification of the IRAs in question in Priv. Ltr. Rul. 199937055 as community property is determined solely under state law. On at least one occasion, however, the Tax Court has held that Code § 408(g) precluded the community spouse from being characterized as a 50 percent distributee of her former husband's IRA and that, therefore, the husband was solely responsible for all tax consequences arising from a distribution from the IRA pursuant to a property settlement decree. *Bunney v. Commissioner,* 114 T.C. No. 17 (2000).

[471] *See, e.g., Stone v. Stone,* 450 F. Supp. 919 (N.D. Cal. 1978), *aff'd,* 632 F.2d 740 (9th Cir. 1980), *cert. denied,* 453 U.S. 922 (1981); *United Ass'n of Journeymen v. Myers,* 488 F. Supp. 704 (M.D. La. 1980), *aff'd on other grounds,* 645 F.2d 532 (5th Cir. 1981); *Employee Savings Plan of Mobil Oil Corp. v. Geer,* 535 F. Supp. 1052 (S.D.N.Y. 1982); *Allard v. Frech,* 754 S.W.2d 111 (Tex. 1988).

payments may be made to the spouse as an alternate payee pursuant to a QDRO, and these payments are not included in determining the 10 percent penalty on premature distributions. In addition, the spouse receiving a distribution pursuant to a QDRO may roll the distribution into an IRA or may elect to have the distribution taxed under special averaging.[472] Finally, the participant and the spouse may use a QDRO to divide the benefits during their lifetimes to give the nonparticipant spouse enough assets to fund a credit shelter trust if he or she is the first to die, if portability is not desired for one reason or another.

In the case of marital dissolution, depending on the participant's circumstances and the provisions of the qualified plan, it may be possible for the QDRO to compel an immediate distribution to the nonparticipant spouse of his or her interest in the plan. In many cases, the nonparticipant spouse should press to have his or her interest distributed as soon as possible. As will be discussed, it may be difficult for the nonparticipant spouse to pass on his or her rights to the plan benefits to heirs or beneficiaries if he or she dies before the participant either dies or begins receiving benefits. By taking an immediate distribution from the participant's plan, the nonparticipant spouse is then free to pass the funds received to his or her heirs or beneficiaries. If the nonparticipant spouse is unable to effect an immediate distribution from the plan, the nonparticipant spouse could consider exchanging his or her interest in the participant's plan benefits for other property.

A QDRO probably cannot be used for purposes of enforcing rights of the heirs or beneficiaries of a nonparticipant spouse who predeceases the participant in the participant's plan benefits. Since Code § 402 taxes the participant on any distributions made pursuant to a QDRO other than to a spouse or a former spouse, it could be concluded that the only other intended recipients would be dependents of the participant. It would seem to be unjust to tax the participant on distributions made to the nonparticipant spouse's children by a prior marriage. In such a situation, however, the participant spouse could elect to have withholding, and at least some of the tax would be paid out of the distribution itself. Finally, under REA, a QDRO can be obtained only by a spouse, a former spouse, or a child or dependent of the participant, not by a former spouse's successors at death.

[472] Priv. Ltr. Rul. 9441004.

The Labor Department has issued two ERISA opinion letters stating that a state's probate court order did not qualify as a QDRO.[473] These opinions are based on a finding that the intent of Congress in developing the QDRO procedure was to assure a greater opportunity for women (whether employees or homemakers) to receive private pension income. According to the Labor Department, the legislative history indicated that in enacting these provisions Congress focused on the division of pension benefits in a marital dissolution or dependent support situation. In addition, the Ninth Circuit Court of Appeals, in *Ablamis* v. *Roper,* held that California's community property law was preempted by ERISA as it applied to the nonparticipant's interest in the participant's qualified retirement plan benefit when the nonparticipant spouse predeceased the participant. Furthermore, the Ninth Circuit held that a probate court order was not a QDRO.[474] Finally, the U.S. Supreme Court, in *Boggs* v. *Boggs,*[475] held that ERISA preempts the Louisiana community property rights of a nonparticipant spouse to transfer his or her community property interest in the plan by his or her will. Further, the preemption extends to property that is distributed from the plan after the death of the nonparticipant spouse, including amounts held in a rollover IRA.

If the participant dies first, the nonparticipant spouse (but not a former spouse) will be entitled to receive either a survivor annuity or the entire accrued benefit of the deceased participant under REA. These rights are not dependent upon community property laws, but upon the express provisions of REA. However, the rights of a former spouse under a QDRO protecting his or her community property interest are superior to the rights of the participant's surviving spouse if the QDRO is in effect prior to the second spouse's rights as a surviving spouse becoming vested, *e.g.,* upon the participant's retirement and election of a qualified joint and last survivor annuity with the current spouse or upon the participant's death.

3. IRAs

Although the Code does not prohibit paying amounts to third parties from an IRA, generally the participant will be subject to income taxation on all distributions from a traditional IRA and the earnings portion of a nonqualified distribution from a Roth IRA. The participant may also be

[473] DOL Opinion Letters No. 90-46A and 90-47 A, December 4, 1990 (*CCH Pension Reporter* ¶ 23,1862).
[474] *Ablamis v. Roper,* 937 F.2d 1450 (9th Cir. 1991).
[475] 520 U.S. 833 (1997).

subject to the 10 percent penalty on premature distributions if a distribution is made before the participant reaches age 59½. An IRA may not be put into the spouse's name during the participant's lifetime, unless pursuant to a divorce.[476] In such a case, the transfer is not taxable and the IRA is treated as the spouse's IRA.

There is no federal law that prevents the heirs or beneficiaries of a nonparticipant spouse from claiming their share of the participant's IRA, and the California Supreme Court upheld such a claim in *Estate of MacDonald*.[477] Such a payment may cause immediate taxation to the participant and, if the participant is under age 59½, a 10 percent penalty. However, in Priv. Ltr. Rul. 8040101, the IRS ruled that the legatees of the nonparticipant spouse were taxed on payments from the participant's IRA. Further, if the IRA is a rollover from a qualified plan that occurred after the death of the nonparticipant spouse, the state law claim will be preempted by ERISA.[478]

Since IRAs are not subject to REA, the participant may designate the beneficiary of his or her own IRA without the consent of the nonparticipant spouse. The nonparticipant spouse, however, may be entitled to claim his or her community property interest after the death of the participant if he or she is not named the beneficiary of at least the amount equal to the community property interest.

4. Estate and Gift Taxes

If the participant spouse dies first, his or her estate includes only half of any benefit in a qualified retirement plan or an IRA, to the extent that the plan benefit or IRA is community property. The other half of the plan benefit or IRA belongs to the nonparticipant spouse, and if the plan benefit or IRA passes at the participant's death to someone other than the nonparticipant spouse, the latter may be deemed to have made a taxable gift. Although Code § 2503(f) exempts from the gift tax the nonparticipant spouse's waiver of the right to benefits granted under REA, it does not apply to the nonparticipant spouse's community property interest in the benefit. However, it is likely that the value of the spouse's REA rights will exceed the spouse's community property interest in the plan benefit. If the

---

[476] Code § 408(d)(6).
[477] 794 P.2d 911 (Cal. 1990).
[478] *Boggs,* discussed *supra*.

nonparticipant spouse is the sole beneficiary of the plan benefit or IRA, there will be no estate tax due either on the participant's share, because of the marital deduction, or on the nonparticipant spouse's share, because he or she has not lost any ownership rights.

A former spouse with a community property interest in a qualified retirement plan benefit who fails to obtain a QDRO before either the participant's death or his or her own death may be deemed to have made a taxable gift of his or her community property interest in the plan. Adequate consideration paid to the nonparticipant spouse will avoid this result.

If the nonparticipant dies before the participant, the nonparticipant's community property interest will be included in his or her gross estate. As a result of the *Boggs* decision, none of the participant's qualified retirement plan benefit or account balance in an IRA that consists of rollovers from the participant's retirement plan should be includible in the nonparticipant's federal gross estate, because he or she has no rights in those assets. If the participant succeeds to the spouse's community property interest either under the spouse's will or automatically based on the theory that the state laws of inheritance are completely preempted by ERISA, then the marital deduction should be available. If the participant or his or her estate is the only person who can receive any benefits under the plan while he or she is alive, a plan benefit payable to a participant who is not currently entitled to receive benefits under the plan should still qualify for the marital deduction, even though it would not satisfy the requirement that income must be payable to the surviving spouse at least annually.[479]

If the nonparticipant spouse does not transfer his or her interest to or for the participant in a manner that qualifies for the marital deduction, the interest will be subject to estate tax. Because the participant is still alive, the estate tax may be payable at a time when the benefit itself is not available. None of the deferral provisions generally available to an estate would be available with respect to the tax on the community property interest in the qualified retirement plan.

[479] TRA 97 § 1311 (a), amending Code § 2056(b)(7), effective for decedents dying after August 5, 1997. The House Committee Report indicates that the law may have been interpreted to obtain the same result before the amendment.

In most cases the spouse should leave his or her interest in qualified retirement plans and IRAs outright to the participant. If this disposition will overfund the marital deduction, an alternative beneficiary should be named; the benefit would then pass to a credit shelter trust or other beneficiary if the participant should disclaim some or all of the benefit.

E. Planning with Respect to Spousal Rights

Spousal rights could have a dramatic impact on the overall estate plan of a participant. In many cases, the tax and nontax objectives of the participant could be thwarted by the refusal of a spouse to consent to a waiver of his or her rights to either the survivor annuity or the participant's vested accrued benefit.

If an individual has any role in the design of a plan, he or she may wish to avoid the survivor annuity rules, including the notice requirements. However, all plans must provide some form of death benefit to the surviving spouse unless the surviving spouse elects otherwise. In the case of a defined contribution plan subject to the qualified survivor annuity rules, the surviving spouse is entitled to a survivor annuity equal to at least 50 percent of the actuarial value of the participant's vested accrued benefit. In the case of a defined contribution plan not subject to the qualified annuity rules, the surviving spouse must be entitled to the entire vested accrued benefit of the participant. In a plan not required to provide the qualified joint and survivor annuity to a married participant, a participant can defeat the nonparticipant spouse's rights to the death benefit required under REA by withdrawing his or her entire benefit in a manner qualifying for rollover treatment, and then transferring the distribution to a traditional IRA. Once the benefit is in the IRA, it is no longer subject to REA, although the IRA may be subject to the domestic relations laws of the state, including the spouse's community property rights.

Spousal rights under REA will impact the drafting and effectiveness of prenuptial and postnuptial agreements. A spouse of a participant may not validly waive his or her rights by signing a prenuptial agreement, since the regulations state that an agreement signed before the marriage is not a valid consent.[480] After the marriage, the spouse will be entitled to his or her rights to the participant's benefits unless he or she consents to another form of distribution. If the spouse refuses to sign the consent even though

[480] Treas. Reg. § 1.401(a)-20, Q&A 28.

required to by a prenuptial agreement, the designated beneficiaries of the participant may have a contractual claim against the spouse under state law. The participant could condition some other form of consideration granted to the spouse under the prenuptial agreement on the spouse's actual consent to the waiver. Unfortunately for the peace of mind of the participant, it may be years after the marriage when the spouse can validly consent to the waiver, since the spouse cannot sign a valid consent to waive his or her right to the qualified joint and survivor annuity until 90 days before the participant's annuity starting date.

In an unpublished case, *Callahan* v. *Hutsell,*[481] the Court of Appeals indicated that a premarital agreement that complied with the consent requirements of REA (specifically, the agreement was in writing, it expressly permitted the participant to designate any beneficiary he or she desired, it acknowledged the effect of the election, and it was witnessed by a notary public) could serve as a valid consent under REA. In this case, the court found that the consent was ineffective because it failed to comply with the plan requirement that it be furnished to the plan administrator. Nevertheless, the court held that even though the premarital agreement did not satisfy the plan requirement, the agreement might still be enforceable against the surviving spouse under state contract law.

The nonparticipant spouse should be advised to seek independent counsel if he or she is asked to consent to a waiver of his or her right to a qualified preretirement survivor annuity, a qualified joint and survivor annuity, or the death benefit under a defined contribution plan exempt from the survivor annuity rules. Independent counsel, however, may not be necessary if the spouse is the sole beneficiary of a trust designated as the beneficiary of the benefits and neither the designation nor the trust agreement may be changed or amended without the consent of the spouse.

If the designated beneficiary is a QTIP trust or a credit shelter trust, the spouse's consent to waive his or her rights should not cause the benefit to be included in his or her estate as a transfer with a retained income interest under Code § 2036(a)(1). Generally, both a QTIP trust and a credit shelter trust should be designed to exclude the assets remaining at the surviving

---

[481] 1993 U.S. App. Lexis 34005 (6th Cir. 1993), *vacating & remanding* 813 F. Supp. 541 (W.D. Ky. 1992).

spouse's death from his or her gross estate. In the case of the QTIP trust, if the election is made, the assets will be includible in the gross estate of the surviving spouse anyway. But if the election is not made and the assets are includible in the estate of the surviving spouse for some other reason, the assets will have been subject to estate tax twice in the same generation.

Chapter Six

Planning

A. Planning Objectives

A participant should focus on the following considerations when planning for distributions from qualified retirement plans and IRAs. First, the participant should consider his or her personal goals when making decisions about the form and timing of benefits during his or her lifetime and beneficiary designations for benefits payable after death. These goals will be restricted by provisions in the plan that may limit both the form and timing of benefit distributions. For example, many defined benefit plans do not permit lump sum distributions. In addition, many plans do not allow (and may not be permitted to allow) a participant to withdraw benefits until the participant reaches his or her early or normal retirement age.

The participant's goals may also be restricted by REA, which requires the consent of the participant's spouse to any beneficiary designation that does not name the spouse as the primary beneficiary of the plan benefit. In addition, except in the case of certain defined contribution plans, REA requires the consent of the participant's spouse to any form of payment during the participant's lifetime other than a qualified joint and survivor annuity.

The second objective should be to avoid the two penalty taxes that may apply to distributions from qualified retirement plans and IRAs. These penalty taxes have been discussed in detail in Chapter Two. The first penalty tax imposes a 10 percent penalty on premature distributions, generally distributions before age 59½ unless an exception applies; the second penalty tax imposes a 50 percent excise tax on the excess of a required minimum distribution over the amount actually distributed during each year after the participant reaches his or her RBD. While it may not always be possible or advisable to avoid the 10 percent penalty on premature distributions, the 50 percent excise tax on undistributed minimum distributions should be avoided in any event, since there is no tax or nontax benefit that will offset this tax. With respect to the 10 percent penalty, the tax-free accumulation of income in the plan or IRA will more than likely offset the penalty if the plan or IRA has existed for even a few years.

The third objective should be to incur the lowest possible income tax on the distribution. For example, a distribution from a qualified retirement plan may be eligible for five-year averaging (if the distribution is made before 2000) or, in the case of a participant who has reached age 50 before January 1, 1986, ten-year averaging or capital gain treatment. In the alternative, the benefit can be left in the plan or rolled into a traditional IRA and paid out over a period of years to avoid a bunching of income in one year. An additional alternative for some individuals is to roll over or convert a traditional IRA to a Roth IRA, incurring taxation of the current balance but allowing future investment earnings to be excluded from taxation. After 2009, any participant in a qualified retirement plan or IRA may convert to a Roth IRA, regardless of his or her AGI.

Deferring the taxable receipt of plan benefits or IRAs for the longest period of time is the fourth objective, provided that the participant can afford to do this (*i.e.,* he or she does not need the plan or IRA assets for current consumption). By deferring the receipt of benefits and IRAs, the participant continues to earn tax-deferred income on the entire benefit or IRA, including the amount that would have been paid in income tax, allowing the amount retained in the plan or IRA to increase more rapidly. Although deferral of qualified retirement plan and traditional IRA benefits may subject some of the benefits to a higher income tax rate if rates are increased, the benefit of tax-free accumulation of income should offset this cost after a few years. Deferral of Roth IRA benefits, assuming that the eventual distributions will be qualified distributions, will not be subject to tax at the projected higher tax rates because they are income-tax free.

As discussed in Chapter Two, under the final regulations dealing with the required minimum distribution rules, the identity of the designated beneficiary at the participant's RBD only affects the applicable distribution period if the spouse is the sole designated beneficiary and is more than ten years younger than the participant.

The fifth objective involves the avoidance or reduction of transfer taxes. Qualifying the benefits for the marital deduction will defer the payment of estate taxes until the death of the surviving spouse. Avoiding irrevocable elections during the client's lifetime will avoid current gift taxes. The transition rule for the estate tax exclusion of benefits under qualified retirement plans may be available if the participant separated from service before 1983, in the case of the unlimited exclusion, or before 1985, in the case of the $100,000 exclusion. Finally, the distribution may be made in whole or part to a credit shelter trust or a beneficiary other than the spouse if the participant does not have sufficient assets outside of plan benefits and IRAs to use up his or her remaining unified credit, if portability is not desired for one reason or another.

B. Planning Before Retirement

1. In General

At the time a person first becomes a participant in a qualified retirement plan or IRA, he or she will be asked to designate a beneficiary to receive any benefits remaining at his or her death. Consequently, when the participant later engages in estate or financial planning, the estate planner should review the existing beneficiary designations to determine whether they are compatible with the recommended estate plan. The estate planner also should review other plan information, including the summary plan description and all benefit statements, particularly the most current statement. The plan document should be obtained, since the summary plan description may not be current or accurate, or may not contain all the options or relevant provisions concerning the payment of benefits. In some cases, the plan document may be out of date, since it may not have been amended to comply with recent changes in the law.[482]

The estate planner should review the participant's overall financial and estate planning objectives, current financial information, and the projected future financial needs of the participant and his or her intended beneficiaries. Periodically, the estate planner should review any new beneficiary designations for plan benefits and IRAs for consistency with the participant's will and other estate planning documents.

2. Beneficiary Designations

In advising the participant with respect to proper beneficiary designations, ethical considerations should be kept in mind. In many cases there may be a need for the spouse to be advised by independent counsel if he or she is asked to sign a consent to a waiver of the qualified preretirement survivor annuity, qualified joint and survivor annuity, or death benefit. In addition, the advisor, regardless of his or her profession, may be incompetent to advise a participant about distributions from qualified retirement plans and

---

[482] *See* Rev. Proc. 97-41, 1997-33 I.R.B. 51.

IRAs because of the complexity in the area or the focus of the advisor's practice. In such a case, the advisor should either associate with a more experienced practitioner with the client's consent or refer the client to such a professional.

The designation of a beneficiary or beneficiaries to receive benefits payable at the death of the participant involves a number of issues. These include whether the benefits will qualify for the marital deduction, whether the benefits may be rolled into an IRA, whether the benefits are taxable, whether ten-year averaging and capital gain treatment if the participant reached age 50 before 1986 is available, whether spousal consent under REA is required, whether the funds may be needed to fund the credit shelter trust, the effect of the designation on the minimum distribution rules, and other practical considerations.

A. The Spouse as Sole Beneficiary

Naming the spouse as the sole beneficiary of a lump sum distribution usually provides greater tax advantages and more flexibility than other designations. If the spouse is named as the beneficiary of a lump sum distribution and the spouse is a citizen of the United States, the benefits will qualify for the marital deduction for estate tax purposes.

The spouse of a deceased participant entitled to a lump sum distribution of the decedent's benefit from a qualified retirement plan may roll the distribution into his or her own IRA. The spouse of a deceased participant also may treat the decedent's IRA as his or her own IRA. In both cases the income tax on the benefit or IRA will be deferred until needed for personal expenses or required to be distributed under the minimum distribution rules. Although the minimum distribution rules allow the spouse to wait until April 1 of the calendar year following the calendar year in which he or she reaches age 70½ to begin receiving distributions from a traditional IRA, any withdrawals made from the IRA before reaching age 59½ will be subject to the 10 percent penalty on premature distributions, unless one of the exceptions applies. The spouse may also designate a beneficiary to receive any benefits remaining at his or her death, increasing the payout period.

On the other hand, if the spouse does not roll the benefits into an IRA or does not treat the decedent's IRA as his or her own, the minimum distribution rules require the spouse to begin receiving distributions when the participant would have reached age 70½. In this case, the 10 percent penalty will not apply to withdrawals before the spouse reaches age 59½. Once the spouse reaches age 59½, a spousal rollover can be made.

The surviving spouse also may elect ten-year averaging and capital gain treatment if the participant reached age 50 before 1986.

If the payment is to be made in a lump sum and the plan is subject to the qualified survivor annuity rules, spousal consent under REA will be required to elect out of both the qualified preretirement survivor annuity and the qualified joint and survivor annuity.

Designating the spouse as the sole beneficiary may result in overfunding the marital deduction if the retirement benefits are a substantial part of the estate. In such a case, the spouse may disclaim the receipt of some or all of the benefits.[483] Designating the spouse as the beneficiary will not provide for institutional management of the benefits distributed unless the spouse engages advisors or transfers the distributed funds to a trust or agency account. Furthermore, the designation of the spouse as the sole beneficiary may not be appropriate if the participant has children by a prior marriage or marriages.

B. Marital Deduction Trust

A trust designed to qualify for the marital deduction (or to be a QDOT) may be designated as beneficiary, either as the primary beneficiary or as a secondary beneficiary, if the spouse disclaims a right to a lump sum distribution. The payment of the benefits to a trust designed to qualify for the marital deduction raises concerns about the nondeductible terminable interest rule.

Designating a trust designed to qualify for the marital deduction is desirable when the participant wants to provide for the needs of his or her spouse during his or her lifetime and to defer the payment of the estate tax on the benefit until the spouse dies, but also wants to control the disposition of any benefit remaining at the spouse's death. Only the QTIP trust (or a charitable remainder trust) will enable the participant to obtain the marital deduction and, at the same time, control the disposition of any benefit or IRA remaining at the spouse's death. A charitable remainder

[483] Priv. Ltr. Rul. 9037048.

trust will only be appropriate if the participant wishes to have the benefit remaining at the death of the surviving spouse payable to a charitable organization. In a life estate general power of appointment trust, the spouse must have the right either during lifetime or at death to give the assets to anyone he or she desires. In an estate trust, any assets remaining in the trust at the death of the surviving spouse must be paid to the surviving spouse's estate, and will therefore be controlled by the surviving spouse's will.

If a trust qualifies for the marital deduction as a QTIP trust or a life estate/general power of appointment trust, the benefits payable to the trust should qualify for the marital deduction if one of two requirements is satisfied. Either the trustee must have the right to withdraw the balance of the benefit at any time and the spouse must have the right to require the trustee to convert unproductive property to productive property, or the spouse must have the right to require the trustee to distribute other assets in an amount equivalent to the income that would have been produced by the undistributed plan benefits and there are other assets in the trust that may be used for this purpose.

If the marital trust is the beneficiary of plan benefits, rollover treatment will be foreclosed unless the spouse has the right to revoke the trust. However, if the participant died after reaching age 59½, the trustee may still elect ten-year averaging and capital gain treatment if the participant reached age 50 before 1986.

Spousal consent will be required under REA, since the benefit is not being paid directly to the spouse or in the form of a survivor annuity. An alternate designation should be made in the event that the spouse should disclaim his or her interest in the benefit. For example, the benefits may then be paid to a credit shelter trust or directly to other beneficiaries. Under the regulations on qualified disclaimers, the spouse may have an income interest in the trust where the disclaimed benefits pass as a result of the disclaimer, but the spouse may not have any discretion over principal distributions of the disclaimed plan benefits unless the exercise of the discretion is subject to an ascertainable standard.

If the surviving spouse or some other individual is not treated as a designated beneficiary under the minimum distribution rules dealing with trusts and the participant dies before the RBD, the entire benefit must be paid out by the end of the year containing the fifth anniversary of the participant's death. These rules are discussed in detail in Section C of Chapter Two. Briefly stated, the following requirements must be satisfied by the beneficiary determination date, which is September 30 of the year following the year of the participant's death, in order for the spouse to be treated as a designated beneficiary:

(1) The trust must be a valid trust or would be a valid trust except for the fact that the trust has no corpus;

(2) The trust must be irrevocable or will, by its terms, become irrevocable upon the death of the participant;

(3) The beneficiaries of the trust entitled to the plan benefits or IRA must be identifiable; and

(4) Certain documentation requirements must be satisfied (which do not have to be satisfied until October 31 of the year following the year of the participant's death).

C. Credit Shelter Trust or Other Beneficiaries

In some cases, a credit shelter trust, if portability is not desired for one reason or another, or individuals other than the spouse should be named as the beneficiary or beneficiaries. This designation is called for when the participant's other assets are insufficient to fund fully the credit shelter amount. If the benefits are paid to a credit shelter trust or an individual other than the participant's surviving spouse, ten-year averaging and capital gain treatment if the participant reached age 50 before 1986 will be available. A nonspousal rollover to an inherited IRA may also be available.

Under REA, the spouse will have to consent to the designation of a credit shelter trust or other individual as the beneficiary to receive the plan benefits. If the spouse has an income interest in the credit shelter trust, the spouse's consent to waive his or her right to a survivor annuity should not cause the part of the credit shelter trust attributable to the benefits to be included in his or her federal gross estate under Code § 2036(a), because the waiver is not treated as a taxable gift by the spouse.

An alternate designation should be made if the trustee disclaims the benefits. For example, the benefits could then be paid to a marital deduction trust or directly to the surviving spouse.

If the maximum deferral of benefit payments is desired, the trust must satisfy the requirements under the minimum distribution rules in order for the oldest beneficiary to be treated as a designated beneficiary; otherwise, the entire benefit must be paid out by the end of the fifth year following the year of the participant's death, if he or she dies before the RBD.

C. Planning at Retirement

Many of the same considerations that apply to planning for beneficiary designations before retirement also apply when a retiring participant is selecting the form of payment and the beneficiary to receive any benefits remaining after his or her death. As discussed in the previous section, the advisor must review all plan information, including the plan document. Income tax and transfer tax consequences may play an important part in the decision-making process at this point.

For example, special income tax treatment may be available if the benefit is paid in a lump sum. A recipient of a distribution with respect to a participant who has reached age 50 before January 1, 1986, may choose one of the following two methods for taxing a lump sum distribution:

(1) Ten-year averaging plus long-term capital gain treatment on the pre-1974 portion (at a 20 percent maximum rate); or

(2) Ten-year averaging on the entire amount.

Distributions from an IRA are not eligible for averaging or capital gain treatment.

If a current distribution of the entire benefit is not desired or available, the payment may be made in installments or in the form of an annuity for the life of the participant or the joint lives of the participant and beneficiary. Payments may come directly from the plan, or a commercial annuity could be purchased and distributed to the participant. If a lump sum distribution is permitted under the plan, the participant should consider a rollover into an IRA, since he or she usually will have more control over the timing of the payments and the investment of the undistributed funds. Leaving the benefits in the plan, however, may give the benefits more protection from the participant's creditors than they would receive in an IRA, depending on federal bankruptcy and state spendthrift laws, as well as protective legislation adopted in many states.

There is generally no reason to leave a qualified retirement plan benefit in the plan instead of transferring it to an IRA if permitted under the plan, unless by leaving the benefit in the plan it will achieve a higher rate of return. Before the 2005 Bankruptcy Abuse Prevention and Consumer Protection Act (the Bankruptcy Act), keeping the benefit in the plan also protected the benefit from creditors. The Supreme Court's decision in *Patterson v. Shumate*[484] upheld the Fourth Circuit's decision that a participant's interest in an ERISA qualified pension plan may be excluded from the participant's bankruptcy estate pursuant to 11 U.S.C. § 541(c)(2).[485] Prior decisions by several federal appellate courts had held that qualified retirement plan benefits could be completely excluded from

---

[484] 504 U.S. 753(1992), *aff'g* 943 F.2d 362(4th Cir. 1991).

[485] What is meant by an "ERISA qualified pension plan" is not entirely clear. *See, e.g., In the Matter of Robert L. Branch*, 16 F.3d 1225(7th Cir. 1994), where the court ruled that a plan in which the only participant was the employer was not an ERISA qualified pension plan because it was not subject to ERISA, citing Labor Regs. § 2510.3-3. *Compare In re Lowenschuss*, 170 F.3d 923(9th Cir. 1999), *cert. denied*, 528 U.S. 877(1999), holding that bankruptcy will not discharge a "debt" created by a state court's divorce order authorizing the division of retirement plan assets as part of a marital property settlement. In that case, the debtor was self-employed and was the sole participant in the retirement plan. The court determined that the plan was not subject to ERISA because only the debtor participated in the plan, and accordingly, the plan could not be "ERISA qualified" under *Patterson v. Shumate*. The court also found that because the divorce court's order gave the debtor's ex-spouse an immediate property right to a percentage of the plan's assets, such percentage could not be included in the debtor's bankruptcy estate. Therefore, the court concluded that the ex-spouse's equitable interest in the plan's assets was not a monetary debt that was dischargeable as part of the debtor's bankruptcy. The court granted the ex-spouse leave to file a request for a qualified domestic relations order (QDRO) with the divorce court to effectuate the distribution of the court's prior award of a property interest in the plan. Although the plan was not subject to ERISA, it presumably was a tax qualified plan, which is also subject to the QDRO rules under § 414(p).

the bankruptcy estate under ERISA's nonalienation prohibition,[486] although other circuits had held otherwise.[487]

An exclusion or exemption for IRAs depended upon state law. However, in 2005, in *Rousey v. Jacoway (In re Rousey),*[488] the Supreme Court held that IRA assets are exempt from the bankruptcy estate to the extent that the assets are reasonably necessary for the support of the debtor and any dependents pursuant to 11 U.S.C. § 522(d)(10)(E). Further, the Bankruptcy Act expanded the protection of IRAs[489] effective for cases commenced 180 days or more after April 20, 2005.[490]

Section 224 of the Bankruptcy Act exempts qualified retirement plan benefits from the bankruptcy estate as long as the plan has received a favorable determination letter or is in substantial compliance with the applicable requirements of the Internal Revenue Code. In addition, such benefits remain exempt if they are rolled into an IRA. Finally, other amounts in an IRA are exempt up to $1,000,000, which is adjusted for inflation every three years (currently $1,245,475, beginning April 1, 2013).[491] Consequently, all qualified retirement plan benefits, and any of such benefits rolled into an IRA, plus up to an additional $1,000,000, as adjusted, of other IRA contributions, are excluded from the bankruptcy estate. However, the same federal exemption does not apply to an inherited IRA, as a result of the Supreme Court's decision in *Clark v. Rameker,*[492] based on the Court's reasoning that an inherited IRA does not qualify as a "retirement fund."

Assuming that the participant's goal is an equal amount of monthly income over a specified number of years and assuming the same rate of return under each method, the following observations can be made. First, larger

---

[486] *See, e.g., In re Moore*, 907 F.2d 1476 (4th Cir. 1990); *In re Lucas*, 924 F.2d 597(6th Cir. 1991), *cert. denied*, 500 U.S. 959 (1991); *Velis v. Kardanis*, 949 F.2d 78 (3d Cir. 1991); *In re Harline*, 950 F.2d 669 (10th Cir. 1991).

[487] *See, e.g., In re Goff*, 706 F.2d 574, 4 EBC 1653 (5th Cir. 1983); *In re Graham*, 726 F.2d 1268 (8th Cir. 1984); *In re Daniel*, 771 F.2d 1352 (9th Cir. 1985); *In re Lichstrahl*, 750 F.2d 1488 (11th Cir. 1985); and *In re Le Feber*, 906 F.2d 330 (7th Cir. 1990).

[488] 125 S. Ct. 1561 (2005).

[489] 2005 Bankruptcy Abuse Prevention and Consumer Protection Act, Pub. L. No. 109-8, § 224. *See* 11 U.S.C. § 522(n).

[490] 2005 Bankruptcy Abuse Prevention and Consumer Protection Act, Pub. L. No. 109-8, § 1501.

[491] Section 104 of the Bankruptcy Code.

[492] 573 U.S. ___, 134 S. Ct. 2242 (2014).

amounts should be rolled into an IRA (or kept in the plan for periodic distributions) rather than being subjected to income tax currently, unless the participant needs a substantial amount of the total benefit at retirement for current consumption.

The second observation is that as the rate of return or payout period increases, the IRA rollover or leave-it-in-the-plan option produces higher after-tax monthly payments. Third, if either the participant's tax bracket increases or Congress increases overall tax rates in the future, taxing the benefit currently using special averaging (and capital gain treatment, if available) may produce a lower overall tax. The benefit of the lower tax rate must be compared to the benefit of the tax-free accumulation of earnings under the deferral option.

The method of distribution must satisfy the required minimum distribution rules to avoid the 50 percent penalty on required distributions that are not actually distributed.

Other considerations that affect the selection of the form of benefit include spousal rights, the financial needs of the participant, the participant's overall estate plan, and the health of the participant, the spouse, and other beneficiaries.

D. Planning After Death

The personal representative of an estate should determine the existence of qualified retirement plan benefits and IRAs in which the decedent was a participant or account holder and should review the plan information and beneficiary designations for all such plans and IRAs, and the amount of benefits payable from each plan or IRA. The personal representative should determine the effect of the decedent's other estate planning documents on the payment of plan benefits and IRAs. These documents will include the decedent's will, any trusts created under the will or outside the will, and any prenuptial or postnuptial agreements, QDROs, and other documents affecting the rights of a surviving spouse or others. The personal representative should determine who the plan administrator or IRA sponsor has determined is entitled to receive the benefits and when Roth IRA benefits will have met the five-year holding period requirement to be nontaxable qualified distributions. If the personal representative believes that the plan administrator or IRA sponsor intends to pay the wrong beneficiary, the personal representative should file a claim and, possibly, seek advice and guidance from the court. If the participant separated from service before 1985, the estate tax exclusion may be available for some or all of the value of the benefits.

As discussed in more detail in Chapter Two, under final regulations dealing with required minimum distributions, the designated beneficiary of a deceased participant is determined as of the beneficiary determination date, which is September 30 of the calendar year following the calendar year of the participant's death. The identity of the designated beneficiary can be affected by a disclaimer by the primary beneficiary or beneficiaries, cashing out one or more beneficiaries, or establishing separate accounts for more than one beneficiary.

Once the advisor has determined the existence and amount of plan benefits and IRAs and the person or persons entitled to them, the advisor should consider whether the person entitled to them should disclaim the benefits, roll the benefits into an IRA if the beneficiary is a spouse, or elect lump sum treatment, if available. A nonspousal beneficiary may consider having a benefit in a qualified retirement plan rolled over into an inherited IRA in order to take advantage of the life expectancy method for determining the required minimum distribution. Finally, a disclaimer of some or all of the benefits may achieve overall transfer and income tax savings.

The advisor should be aware of the implications of having the benefits taxed as IRD. For example, the advisor should caution against using the benefits to satisfy pecuniary bequests, including a pecuniary marital deduction formula bequest, since such a transfer may cause immediate recognition of income. Also, the IRD deduction for estate taxes attributable to the IRD may be available to reduce the taxable portion of the distribution. Finally, estate and trust accounting issues should be considered, since in many cases distributions to a trust will consist of both principal and income. Generally, if the participant has not otherwise directed in the trust agreement, local law will offer some guidance as to the proper characterization of a distribution.

APPENDIX A

Uniform Lifetime Table

Age of the Participant	Distribution Period	Applicable Percentage
70	27.4	3.65%
71	26.5	3.77%
72	25.6	3.91%
73	24.7	4.05%
74	23.8	4.20%
75	22.9	4.37%
76	22.0	4.54%
77	21.2	4.72%
78	20.3	4.93%
79	19.5	5.13%
80	18.7	5.35%
81	17.9	5.59%
82	17.1	5.85%
83	16.3	6.13%
84	15.5	6.45%
85	14.8	6.76%
86	14.1	7.09%
87	13.4	7.46%
88	12.7	7.87%
89	12.0	8.33%
90	11.4	8.77%
91	10.8	9.26%
92	10.2	9.80%
93	9.6	10.42%
94	9.1	10.99%
95	8.6	11.63%
96	8.1	12.35%
97	7.6	13.16%
98	7.1	14.08%
99	6.7	14.93%
100	6.3	15.87%
101	5.9	16.95%
102	5.5	18.18%
103	5.2	19.23%
104	4.9	20.41%
105	4.5	22.22%
106	4.2	23.81%
107	3.9	25.64%
108	3.7	27.03%
109	3.4	29.41%
110	3.1	32.26%
111	2.9	34.48%
112	2.6	38.46%
113	2.4	41.67%
114	2.1	47.62%
115 & older	1.9	52.63%

NOTE: The distribution period is the joint and last survivor expectancy of an individual with an age in the first column and a beneficiary 10 years younger than the participant. The applicable percentage, which is not included in the final regulations but is shown here for illustration purposes, is the percentage, rounded to two decimal places, determined by dividing the distribution period into 100. This is the percentage of a participant's plan benefit or IRA balance that must be distributed by the end of each distribution calendar year, except the distribution for the first distribution calendar year, which can be deferred until April 1 of the following calendar year. The actual number from the table in the regulation should be used when calculating the minimum distribution. However, if the participant's sole designated beneficiary is a spouse who is more than ten years younger than the participant, the applicable distribution period is their joint and last survivor expectancy, determined each year, while both of them are alive. The joint and last survivor expectancy is determined under the Joint and Survivor Table contained in Treas. Reg. § 1.402(a)(9)-9, A-3.

APPENDIX B

Single Life Table

Age	Distribution Period
0	82.4
1	81.6
2	80.6
3	79.7
4	78.7
5	77.7
6	76.7
7	75.8
8	74.8
9	73.8
10	72.8
11	71.8
12	70.8
13	69.9
14	68.9
15	67.9
16	66.9
17	66.0
18	65.0
19	64.0
20	63.0
21	62.1
22	61.1
23	60.1
24	59.1
25	58.2
26	57.2
27	56.2
28	55.3
29	54.3
30	53.3
31	52.4
32	51.4
33	50.4
34	49.4
35	48.5
36	47.5
37	46.5

Age	Distribution Period
38	45.6
39	44.6
40	43.6
41	42.7
42	41.7
43	40.7
44	39.8
45	38.8
46	37.9
47	37.0
48	36.0
49	35.1
50	34.2
51	33.3
52	32.3
53	31.4
54	30.5
55	29.6
56	28.7
57	27.9
58	27.0
59	26.1
60	25.2
61	24.4
62	23.5
63	22.7
64	21.8
65	21.0
66	20.2
67	19.4
68	18.6
69	17.8
70	17.0
71	16.3
72	15.5
73	14.8
74	14.1
75	13.4

Age	Distribution Period
76	12.7
77	12.1
78	11.4
79	10.8
80	10.2
81	9.7
82	9.1
83	8.6
84	8.1
85	7.6
86	7.1
87	6.7
88	6.3
89	5.9
90	5.5
91	5.2
92	4.9
93	4.6
94	4.3
95	4.1
96	3.8
97	3.6
98	3.4
99	3.1
100	2.9
101	2.7
102	2.5
103	2.3
104	2.1
105	1.9
106	1.7
107	1.5
108	1.4
109	1.2
110	1.1
over 110	1.0

NOTE: This table is contained in Treas. Reg. § 1.401(a)(9)-9, A-1. Under the minimum distribution rules, this table is used for determining the life expectancy of a participant who dies after the RBD if there is no designated beneficiary by September 30 of the calendar year following the participant's death (or if the designated beneficiary's life expectancy is shorter than the participant's), or the life expectancy of the participant's designated beneficiary after the participant's death (regardless of whether the participant dies before or after the RBD) if there is a designated beneficiary by September 30 of the calendar year following the participant's death (unless the participant dies after the RBD and the participant's life expectancy is longer than the designated beneficiary's life expectancy). See the chart in Exhibit D for when the life expectancy of an individual is determined (or, in the case of a spouse, redetermined each year).

APPENDIX C

Abbreviated Joint and Survivor Table

Age of P	Age of S	J&S EX	Table
70	45	39.4	27.4
70	46	38.6	27.4
70	47	37.7	27.4
70	48	36.8	27.4
70	49	35.9	27.4
71	45	39.4	26.5
71	46	38.5	26.5
71	47	37.6	26.5
71	48	36.7	26.5
71	49	35.9	26.5
72	45	39.3	25.6
72	46	38.4	25.6
72	47	37.5	25.6
72	48	36.6	25.6
72	49	35.8	25.6

Age of P	Age of S	J&S EX	Table
73	45	39.3	24.7
73	46	38.4	24.7
73	47	37.5	24.7
73	48	36.6	24.7
73	49	35.7	24.7
74	45	39.2	23.8
74	46	38.3	23.8
74	47	37.4	23.8
74	48	36.5	23.8
74	49	35.6	23.8
75	45	39.2	22.9
75	46	38.3	22.9
75	47	37.4	22.9
75	48	36.5	22.9
75	49	35.6	22.9

Age of P	Age of S	J&S EX	Table
76	45	39.1	22.0
76	46	38.2	22.0
76	47	37.3	22.0
76	48	36.4	22.0
76	49	35.5	22.0
77	45	39.1	21.2
77	46	38.2	21.2
77	47	37.3	21.2
77	48	36.4	21.2
77	49	35.5	21.2
78	45	39.1	20.3
78	46	38.2	20.3
78	47	37.2	20.3
78	48	36.3	20.3
78	49	35.4	20.3

Age of P	Age of S	J&S EX	Table
79	45	39.1	19.5
79	46	38.1	19.5
79	47	37.2	19.5
79	48	36.3	19.5
79	49	35.4	19.5
80	45	39.0	18.7
80	46	38.1	18.7
80	47	37.2	18.7
80	48	36.3	18.7
80	49	35.4	18.7

"P" refers to Participant.

"S" refers to Spouse.

"J&S EX" refers to the joint and survivor expectancy multiple.

"Table" refers to the applicable distribution period under the Uniform Lifetime Table (see Appendix A).

Note: This table is contained in Treas. Reg. § 1.401(a)(9)-9, A-3, Joint and Last Survivor Table. Under the minimum distribution rules, this table is used in lieu of the Uniform Lifetime Table set forth in Appendix A for determining the joint and last survivor expectancy of the participant and the participant's spouse if the spouse is more than 10 years younger than the participant and is named as the participant's sole designated beneficiary during the entire year. The applicable distribution period from the Uniform Lifetime Table is provided for comparison. Of course, this table only covers a participant age 70 to 80 having a spouse who is age 45 to 49. See the actual table contained in the regulations for other age combinations.

APPENDIX D

Chart for Determining Applicable Distribution Period

Designated Beneficiary	Applicable Distribution Period at RBD	Applicable Distribution Period if P dies before RBD	Applicable Distribution Period if P dies after RBD
P's Spouse is not P's sole DB	**1** Table	**2** DB's L EX, determined in the year following the year of P's death, reduced by 1 for each year thereafter	**3** The longer of the period determined in box 2 or 9
P's sole DB is P's Spouse	**4** Table, or, if S is more than 10 years younger than P, J&S redetermined each year (if Spouse no longer P's sole DB at end of a calendar year, the Table must be used unless the spouse died or there was a divorce and P did not name a new beneficiary before the end of that year)	**5** S's L EX, beginning in the year P would have reached age 70½, redetermined each year until S's death, when it becomes S's L EX in the year of death, reduced by 1 for each year that elapses after the year of S's death **(consider spousal rollover)**	**6** S's L EX, redetermined each year until S's death, when it becomes S's L EX in the year of death, reduced by 1 for each year that elapses after the year of S's death **(consider spousal rollover)**
No DB	**7** Table	**8** By the end of the 5th calendar year following the calendar year of P's death	**9** P's L Ex determined in the year of P's death, reduced by 1 for each year thereafter

RBD = Required beginning date, which for all account holders of IRAs and participants in qualified retirement plans who own more than 5 percent of the sponsoring employee is April 1 following the year in which the Participant reaches age 70½. For participants in qualified retirement plans who do not own more than 5 percent of the sponsoring employer, unless the plan applies the rule in the first sentence to all employees, the RBD is April 1 of the calendar year following the later of the calendar year in which the Participant retires or reaches age 70½.

Table = The Uniform Lifetime Table. See Appendix A.

P = Participant, which includes a participant in a qualified retirement plan or an account holder in an IRA.

S = Spouse of the Participant, who, depending upon the context, may be the Participant's surviving spouse. Note that unless the Spouse is the Participant's sole Designated Beneficiary, the Spouse is treated as any other Designated Beneficiary. The Spouse will be the Participant's sole Designated Beneficiary to the extent that he or she is the outright beneficiary of some or all of the Participant's plan benefit or IRA. If the Spouse is one of two or more Designated Beneficiaries, he or she will not be treated as the Participant's sole Designated Beneficiary unless by September 30 of the calendar year following the calendar year of the Participant's death a separate account is created for S's portion of the plan benefit or IRA, the other Designated Beneficiary disclaims his or her interest, or the other Designated Beneficiary's portion is distributed to him or her. If the beneficiary is a trust and the Spouse is a beneficiary of the trust, he or she will be treated as the Participant's sole Designated Beneficiary only if all distributions from the plan or IRA paid to the trust during his or her lifetime are required to be redistributed to him or her. In addition, to the extent the Spouse has the right to the plan benefit or IRA either as the outright beneficiary or a beneficiary of a trust who has the right to withdraw the right to receive the plan benefit or IRA, the Spouse may have the Participant's plan benefit (if permitted under the plan) or IRA rolled over or transferred to his or her own IRA or, if named as the outright beneficiary, may elect to treat the Participant's IRA as his or her own IRA, in which case, the required minimum distribution rules will now apply treating the Spouse as the Participant.

DB = Designated Beneficiary, which, in most cases, must be established by September 30 of the year following the year of the Participant's death, except when the Participant names his or her Spouse as his or her sole Designated Beneficiary, and the Spouse is more than 10 years younger than the Participant. In this case, the identity of the Designated Beneficiary is relevant at the Participant's RBD. Note that an individual beneficiary of a trust named as the Participant's beneficiary may be treated as the Participant's Designated Beneficiary if the trust satisfies the first three of the four requirements discussed in the outline by September 30 of the calendar year following the calendar year of the Participant's death and the documentation requirements by October 31 of the calendar year following the calendar year of the participant's death or, if the Participant's Spouse is the Participant's sole Designated Beneficiary and is more than 10 years younger than the Participant, the four requirements are satisfied at the beginning of the calendar year of the distribution. Note also that the Designated Beneficiary must be an individual who is named by the Participant in a beneficiary designation form or under the terms of the plan or IRA.

J&S = Joint and survivor expectancy of the Participant and Spouse redetermined ("recalculated") each year, which can only be the applicable distribution period if both the Participant and the Spouse are alive, the Spouse is more than 10 years younger than the Participant, and the Participant has named the Spouse as his or her sole Designated Beneficiary.

LEX = Life expectancy of the Designated Beneficiary, which may include a Spouse.

NOTE: except in the case of P's death before the RBD when S is the sole Designated Beneficiary, distributions to the DB after P's death must commence by December 31 of the calendar year following the calendar year of P's death.

APPENDIX E

Illustration of Tax Consequences

Mrs. Smith, a widow, has accumulated $2 million in a pension plan. She dies in 2015 at age 65, survived by all her children and a grandchild. She was a resident of a state that has no estate or income tax. She has designated a trust that is held exclusively for the benefit of her grandchild whose parents are both alive as the recipient of the plan benefit, which is to be paid in a lump sum. The grandchild's interest in the trust is vested and will be included in the grandchild's federal gross estate.

Mrs. Smith's federal gross estate is $10 million, and therefore the marginal federal estate tax rate is 40 percent. The generation-skipping transfer (GST) tax rate is also 40 percent. The trust's marginal federal income tax rate is 39.6 percent (for federal income tax purposes, taxable income of a trust in excess of $12,300 is taxed at 39.6% in 2015). Mrs. Smith had used her GST exemption before her death. Assume that Mrs. Smith's will contains a tax apportionment clause that reduces a bequest by any estate and GST taxes attributable to the bequest.

<u>Calculation of Applicable Taxes</u>

Value of benefit passing to Grandchild's Trust before any taxes	$2,000,000
Estate tax rate	40%
Federal estate tax	$800,000
Amount passing to Grandchild's Trust after estate taxes ($2,000,000 – $800,000)	$1,200,000

Because the GST tax in the case of a direct skip is tax exclusive (*i.e.*, it is determined by applying the 40 percent GST tax rate to the amount passing after the GST tax), the GST tax can be determined by applying the following formula:

Amount passing to the recipient before the GST tax minus amount passing to the recipient before the GST tax divided by 1 + GST tax rate equals the GST tax:	
$1,200,000 divided by 1.40 (1+ GST tax rate) =	$857,143
$1,200,000 – $857,143 =	$342,857
Amount subject to income tax ($2,000,000 less the IRD deduction of $1,142,857, which is the sum of the GST tax ($342,857) and the federal estate tax ($800,000)	$857,143
Federal income tax rate	39.6%
Federal income tax	$339,428
Amount left	$517,716

<u>Summary of Taxes</u>

Original amount	$2,000,000
Federal estate tax	($800,000)
GST tax	($342,857)
Combined federal and state income tax	($339,425)
Total taxes	($1,482,285)
Amount left (about 25 percent of the original $2,000,000 bequest)	$517,716

APPENDIX F

Sample Forms

The following sample beneficiary designation forms and trust language forms are merely suggestions and should not be used unless the drafter fully understands the rules applicable to distributions from qualified retirement plans and IRAs. State law must be considered for IRAs, since state law may affect the interpretation of the IRA beneficiary designation forms and may give a surviving spouse or other individual certain rights with respect to a participant's benefit in an IRA. The I.R.C. and ERISA provisions granting to a surviving spouse rights in the participant's qualified retirement plan benefits must also be considered. In the case of a qualified retirement plan benefit, because the spouse is not the beneficiary and the form of payment is not a qualified preretirement survivor annuity, beneficiary designation Forms II, III, and IV must have the consent of the participant's spouse, in writing, which must be either notarized or witnessed by a plan representative. The participant's spouse must also consent to Form I in the case of a qualified retirement plan benefit other than a defined contribution plan that is exempt from the qualified preretirement survivor annuity requirements, since the payment will be made in a lump sum rather than in the form of a survivor annuity. Finally, the plan itself must be reviewed carefully to be sure that the desired beneficiary designation is permitted under the plan.

Form I, which provides for an outright distribution of the plan benefit or IRA to the surviving spouse, will be used most often, particularly when there is a stable marriage and the participant has sufficient assets to fund a credit shelter trust or is relying on portability to use his or her applicable exclusion amount. Form II will be used where the participant wishes to provide for the surviving spouse during his or her lifetime and qualify the benefit or IRA for the marital deduction, but wants to retain as much of the benefit as possible to pass to the participant's children by a prior marriage or other beneficiaries. Form II should satisfy the IRS's ruling position concerning qualifying plan benefits and IRAs payable to a QTIP trust for the marital deduction.

Form III will be used when the plan benefit is the asset that will fund the credit shelter trust. Note that this form can be combined with the other forms when only a portion of the plan benefit or IRA is required to fund the credit shelter trust. The beneficiary designation may be made to a trust before it is divided into two trusts, one designed to qualify for the marital deduction and one designed to be a credit shelter trust. In such a case, the trust will usually have a formula to determine the percentage of the trust assets to be allocated to each trust. As long as the individual beneficiaries entitled to the plan benefit or IRA are identifiable by September 30 of the calendar year following the calendar year in which the participant died, the rule that the beneficiaries entitled to the plan benefit or IRA be identifiable will be satisfied. If all distributions made to the trust are not required to be paid to the spouse during his or her lifetime, then payments of the plan benefit or IRA would have to commence by December 31 of the calendar year following the calendar year of the participant's death and must be made over the surviving spouse's life expectancy, determined in the year following the year of the participant's death, reduced by one year for each year thereafter. If some of the plan benefit or IRA is allocated by the spouse as the executor or trustee, or under a power given to him or her by the participant, to a marital trust that gives the spouse a power to withdraw all of the principal, the surviving spouse may be able to withdraw the benefit or IRA and roll it into his or her own IRA.[1] The final beneficiary form deals with a bequest to a charitable organization. The two sample trust language forms are designed to qualify the plan benefit or IRA for the marital deduction. The forms are not meant to exhaust all the possible beneficiary designations a participant may wish to consider. As with any sample forms, there is no guarantee that these forms are appropriate in any particular case or that they satisfy applicable federal or state law.

---

[1] *See* Mezzullo, "Recent Letter Rulings Provide Post-Mortem Planning Opportunities for Retirement Benefits," 4 *Taxation of Employee Benefits* (No. 2, July/August 1996).

FORM I: BENEFICIARY DESIGNATION FOR QUALIFIED RETIREMENT PLAN BENEFIT OR INDIVIDUAL RETIREMENT ACCOUNT NAMING SURVIVING SPOUSE AS PRIMARY BENEFICIARY AND TRUST AS SECONDARY BENEFICIARY

My [benefit or IRA] shall be distributed in a lump sum to my [husband or wife] if my [husband or wife] survives me and does not disclaim [his or her] right to receive the [benefit or IRA]. If my [husband or wife] does not survive me, or if my [husband or wife] survives me but disclaims [his or her] right to receive all or a portion of such [benefit or IRA] pursuant to a qualified disclaimer as defined in I.R.C. § 2518(b) or (c)(3), my [benefit or IRA] or portion that is disclaimed shall be distributed to the trustee of the family trust created under the trust created by me as of ________________, in installments, payable at least annually, equal to the amount required to be distributed under the minimum distribution rules under I.R.C. § 401(a)(9) and the regulations thereunder, or any subsequent statute requiring minimum distributions from such [plans or IRAs]. If the [benefit or IRA] is payable to a trust, my trustee shall have the right at any time to withdraw all or any part of the remaining [benefit or IRA] or to designate a beneficiary of the trust to receive any remaining payments directly and to have the right to withdraw at any time all or any part of the remaining [benefit or IRA].

NOTE: If a trustee is also a beneficiary, the participant may want to restrict the right of the trustee to designate a beneficiary of the trust to have the right to withdraw the remaining benefits to avoid inclusion of the benefit or IRA in the beneficiary's federal gross estate because he or she has a general power of appointment over the benefit or IRA. This same comment applies to Forms II, III, and VI.

FORM II: BENEFICIARY DESIGNATION FOR QUALIFIED RETIREMENT PLAN BENEFIT OR INDIVIDUAL RETIREMENT ACCOUNT NAMING QTIP TRUST AS PRIMARY BENEFICIARY AND FAMILY TRUST AS SECONDARY BENEFICIARY

If my [husband or wife] survives me, my [benefit or IRA] shall be distributed to the QTIP trust created under the ____________ trust created by me as of ____________, in installments, payable at least annually, equal to the amount required to be distributed under the minimum distribution rules under I.R.C. § 401(a)(9) and the regulations thereunder, or any subsequent statute requiring minimum distributions from such [plans or IRAs]. If my [husband or wife] does not survive me, my [benefit or IRA] shall be distributed to the trustee of the family trust created under the trust created by me as of ________________, in installments, payable at least annually, equal to the amount required to be distributed under the minimum distribution rules under I.R.C. § 401(a)(9) and the regulations thereunder, or any subsequent statute requiring minimum distributions from such [plans or IRAs]. My trustee shall have the right at any time to withdraw any part or all of the remaining [benefit or IRA] or to designate a beneficiary of the trust to receive any remaining payments directly or to have the right to withdraw at any time all or part of the remaining [benefit or IRA].

NOTE: The plan benefit or IRA should qualify for the marital deduction as long as the spouse has the right to require that any unproductive property be converted into productive property and any income generated or deemed to be generated by the plan benefit or IRA be withdrawn from the plan or IRA and distributed to him or her and the trustee has the right to accelerate payments from the plan or IRA. *See* Treas. Reg. § 20.2056(b)-5(f)(4); Treas. Reg. § 1.401(a)(9)-5, A-7(c)(3), *Examples 1 and 2*; and Rev. Rul. 2006-26. See comment to Form I concerning the trustee's right to designate a beneficiary to have the right to withdraw the remaining benefit or IRA.

FORM III: BENEFICIARY DESIGNATION FOR QUALIFIED RETIREMENT PLAN BENEFIT OR INDIVIDUAL RETIREMENT ACCOUNT NAMING CREDIT SHELTER TRUST AS PRIMARY BENEFICIARY

My [benefit or IRA] shall be distributed to the ___________ trust created by me as of ________________, in installments equal to the amount required to be distributed under the minimum distribution rules under I.R.C. § 401(a)(9) and the regulations thereunder, or any subsequent statute requiring minimum distributions from such [plans or IRAs]. My trustee shall have the right at any time to withdraw all or any part of the remaining [benefit or IRA] or to designate a beneficiary of the trust to receive any remaining payments directly and to have the right to withdraw at any time all or any part of the remaining [benefit or IRA].

NOTE: See comment to Form I concerning the trustee's right to designate a beneficiary to have the right to withdraw the remaining benefit or IRA.

FORM IV: DESIGNATION OF A CHARITABLE BENEFICIARY TO RECEIVE BENEFITS UNDER A QUALIFIED RETIREMENT PLAN OR IRA

I direct that [all or ______ percent] of my [benefit or IRA] be distributed in a lump sum to the XYZ charitable organization.

NOTE: As long as the charity's interest in the plan benefit or IRA is paid to the charity or is segregated into a separate account or separate share before September 30 of the calendar year following the calendar year of the participant's death, the charity will not be treated as a beneficiary of the remaining portion of a plan benefit or IRA, and, therefore, will not cause the deceased participant not to have a designated beneficiary.

FORM V: PROVISION IN TRUST AGREEMENT WHEN TRUSTEE OF A TRUST IS GIVEN THE RIGHT UNDER A QUALIFIED RETIREMENT PLAN OR IRA BENEFICIARY DESIGNATION TO ACCELERATE WITHDRAWALS TO QUALIFY FOR THE MARITAL DEDUCTION

My [husband or wife] shall have the right to direct my trustee of the marital trust to make any unproductive property productive or to convert any unproductive property into income-producing property within a reasonable time. In lieu of making the property productive or converting the unproductive property, my trustee may distribute quarterly to my [husband or wife] other assets from the marital trust the value of which is equal to the income that would have been produced during the calendar quarter if the property had been made productive or converted into income-producing property. Unproductive property shall include any benefit held in a qualified retirement plan as defined in I.R.C. § 401(a), any qualified retirement annuity as defined in I.R.C. § 403(a) or 403(b), and any individual retirement account as defined in I.R.C. § 408(a), but only if and to the extent that income generated or deemed to be generated by the plan benefit, annuity, or account is not distributed to the trust at least annually or the assets in the separate account or share representing the plan benefit, annuity, or account are not producing adequate income, and the withdrawal of such income (or deemed income) from the plan or IRA and distribution of such amount to my [husband or wife] shall be deemed to satisfy my [husband's or wife's] right granted in this paragraph.

FORM VI: PROVISION IN TRUST AGREEMENT TO BE INCLUDED IN DIRECTIONS TO TRUSTEE TO QUALIFY FOR THE MARITAL DEDUCTION

I direct my trustee to treat distributions from any qualified retirement plan as defined in I.R.C. § 401(a), any qualified retirement annuity as defined in I.R.C. § 403(a) or 403(b), or any individual retirement account as defined in I.R.C. § 408(a) as income of the trust to the extent that the distribution represents income generated or deemed to be generated by such plan, annuity, or individual retirement account, notwithstanding the treatment of such portion of the distribution under any law concerning the determination of income and principal for trust accounting purposes and my trustee shall not charge to such income any expense properly chargeable to the nonincome portion of the distribution. In addition, my trustee shall have the right in his or her or its sole discretion to withdraw any part or all of the remaining qualified plan benefit, annuity, or individual retirement account or to direct that the plan benefit, annuity, or individual retirement account be paid directly to the beneficiary of the trust who is entitled to the income of the trust and to give such beneficiary the right to withdraw at any time all or any part of the benefit, annuity, or individual retirement account.

NOTE: If the beneficiary is also the trustee, the trustee should not be given the right to give the beneficiary the right to withdraw, since such a right would be treated as a general power of appointment for transfer tax purposes.

APPENDIX G

Hypothetical Retirement Plan Scenarios

PART I

Mary Smith is a participant in a money purchase pension plan sponsored by the Good Products Company, where she has been an employee for more than 40 years. She is currently a corporate officer and owns more than 5 percent of the stock of Good Products Company. She has no intention of retiring as long as her health, which is currently excellent, permits her to work. She has participated in the Good Products Company Money Purchase Pension Plan for 25 years. Her 66th birthday was May 29, 2015. She has come to you on December 15, 2015, for advice on naming a beneficiary to receive benefits if she dies before her required beginning date (RBD) (April 1, 2020). Fifty percent of the value of her benefit is currently payable to her husband, John, in the form of a qualified preretirement survivor annuity, as required under the Code and ERISA, and the balance is payable to her estate under the plan's default rule. The value of her accrued benefit as of December 31, 2014, was $1,500,000.

Mary has been happily married to John for 40 years. They do not contemplate that their relationship will ever change. John is a retired sales representative, who was a participant in a defined benefit plan sponsored by the personal service corporation he owned. He received his benefit under the plan in the form of a lump sum distribution at age 60, when he liquidated the corporation. He elected to roll the entire distribution into an individual retirement account. The balance in his IRA is currently $800,000. John, who is about three years younger than Mary, reached age 63 on January 15, 2015. Mary and John have one child, Anne, who reached age 35 in 2015. Both Mary and John are U.S. citizens.

QUESTION I-1.

If Mary has other assets to fund a credit shelter trust, who should be the beneficiary of her plan benefit?

ANSWER:

Mary should name John as her beneficiary. This will be the most appropriate choice in situations where the client is happily married and has sufficient assets other than qualified retirement plan benefits and IRAs to fund a credit shelter trust or will rely on portability to use his or her applicable exclusion amount. Naming the spouse as the beneficiary gives the surviving spouse a number of options and defers the payment of estate tax until the death of the surviving spouse. The following are considerations when naming John as a beneficiary of a lump sum payment or giving him the right to withdraw all of the plan benefit at any time.

1. The payment of the plan benefit in a lump sum to John (since he is a citizen of the United States) will qualify the benefit for the marital deduction for estate tax purposes.

    a. The same result will be achieved if John leaves the benefit in the plan, but he has the right to withdraw the entire benefit at any time.

2. If the plan permits a lump sum distribution, John may roll the plan benefit into his own IRA, thereby deferring payment of income tax on the plan benefit.

    a. He can wait until April 1 of the calendar year following the calendar year in which he reaches age 70½ to begin receiving distributions from his IRA.

    b. If John were younger, any withdrawals from the IRA before he reached age 59½ would be subject to the 10 percent additional income tax unless an exception applied.

        (1) If he had not rolled the plan benefit into his own IRA, and instead had taken withdrawals from the plan, the 10 percent additional income tax would not apply to withdrawals before he reached age 59½.

    c. John may also name a beneficiary, such as his daughter Anne, to receive the balance in the IRA remaining at his death.

d. John will also have the option to roll the benefit from his traditional IRA into a Roth IRA.

   (1) That action would cause the benefit to be currently taxed, but could shelter all future earnings from income tax and avoid minimum distributions while John is living.

3. If Mary had reached age 50 before 1986, John could also elect ten-year averaging and capital gain treatment for a distribution qualifying as a lump sum distribution. Note that five-year averaging is no longer available after 1999.

4. Because the benefit is in a money purchase pension plan, John's consent under the Retirement Equity Act (REA) will be required to elect out of the qualified preretirement survivor annuity if the benefit is to be paid in a lump sum after Mary's death.

5. Designating John as the sole beneficiary may result in overfunding the marital deduction if the plan benefit is a substantial part of Mary's estate, in which case John may disclaim the receipt of some or all of the benefit if appropriate.

6. Under the minimum distribution rules, if Mary dies before her RBD, and John does not roll over the benefit to his own IRA, the payments do not have to commence until Mary would have reached age 70½ if the benefit is left in the plan.

   a. John may also name a new beneficiary and if he dies before payments must commence, the payments may be made over the beneficiary's life or life expectancy.

   b. John will still be able to roll any remaining benefits in excess of the required minimum distribution into his own IRA, even after payments must commence.

7. Designating John as the beneficiary of a lump sum distribution will not provide for professional management of the funds unless he engages advisors or transfers the funds to a trust with someone else as trustee.

8. Designating John as the sole beneficiary might not be appropriate if Mary had children by prior marriages.

QUESTION I-2.

If Mary does not have any other assets to fund a credit shelter trust, who should be the beneficiary?

ANSWER:

In this situation, Mary could either rely on portability to use her applicable exclusion amount or name a trust designed to be excluded from John's gross estate as the beneficiary of her benefit to the extent necessary to take full advantage of the applicable exclusion amount ($5,430,000 in 2015). Mary could name a trust as the beneficiary of her plan benefit that, upon her death, will be divided into two shares. One share, which would equal the excess of any plan benefit not required to take advantage of the applicable exclusion amount, would be paid either outright to John or to a trust designed to qualify for the marital deduction. The other share would be paid to a trust that would be a typical credit shelter trust. Because John would be the income/current distribution beneficiary of both the marital deduction trust and the credit shelter trust and assuming that all remainder beneficiaries will be individuals younger than John, such as descendants of Mary and John, it should be possible to have the plan benefit payable to the trusts over his life expectancy. Unless all distributions to the trust are required to be redistributed to John during his lifetime, John will not be treated as the sole designated beneficiary. Consequently, payments cannot be deferred until Mary would have reached age 70½; they must be paid out over John's life expectancy, determined in the year following the year in which Mary dies, reduced by one year for each year thereafter. John may roll any of the plan benefit going to him outright into his own IRA. In addition, he may roll the portion of the plan benefit payable to the marital deduction trust into his own IRA if he has the discretion as executor or trustee to allocate the plan benefit to the marital deduction trust or it is automatically allocated to the marital deduction trust pursuant to the formula and he has the right to withdraw the balance payable to the marital deduction trust. John could then wait until his required beginning date before beginning to receive the plan benefit. In most cases, naming John as the primary beneficiary, with a credit shelter trust as the alternate beneficiary, will give John the opportunity to decide at Mary's death whether the transfer tax benefit of a credit shelter trust outweighs the income tax benefit of a rollover of the entire benefit to John's own IRA.

In order to have a beneficiary of a trust treated as a designated beneficiary for purposes of the minimum distribution rules, the regulations require the trust to satisfy the following four requirements, generally by September 30 of the year following the year of the participant's death:

1. The trust must be a valid trust or would be a valid trust under state law if it had a corpus.

2. The beneficiaries of the trust entitled to the plan benefits or IRAs must be identifiable.

3. The trust must be either irrevocable or, by its terms, will become irrevocable at the participant's death.

4. The documentation requirements must be satisfied (this requirement needs to be satisfied by October 31 of the year following the year of the participant's death).

If the participant's designated beneficiary at his or her RBD is his or her spouse, and the spouse is more than 10 years younger than the participant, then these requirements must be satisfied at the participant's RBD in order to treat John as Mary's sole beneficiary. Under the documentation requirements, the participant or the trustee must furnish to the plan administrator by October 31 of the calendar year following the year of the participant's death (or the participant's RBD if the participant's designated beneficiary is a spouse more than ten years younger than the participant) either the trust instrument or a list of beneficiaries, including contingent and remainder beneficiaries, and the conditions on their entitlement. In addition, the participant or trustee must certify that the list is complete and agree to furnish a copy of the trust agreement upon demand. If the designated beneficiary at the participant's RBD is a spouse more than ten years younger than the participant, then the participant must also agree to furnish any amendment to the trust or an updated certification, if the amendment changes any of the information in the certification.

If the trust fails to satisfy these requirements or if any of the identified beneficiaries of the trust may not be designated beneficiaries, the participant will be treated as having no designated beneficiary. In such a case, the entire benefit or IRA would have to be paid out by the end of the year containing the fifth anniversary of the participant's death if the participant died before his or her RBD; if the participant dies after his or her RBD, payments must be made only over his or her remaining life expectancy, determined in the year of his or her death, and reduced by one year for each year thereafter.

The following additional considerations must be kept in mind if the credit shelter trust is named as the beneficiary.

1. The marital deduction will not be available.

2. Rollover treatment will not be available.

3. If Mary had reached age 50 before 1986, ten-year averaging and capital gain treatment would be available if the distribution qualified as a lump sum distribution. Note that five-year averaging is no longer available after 1999.

4. John's consent to waive his rights under REA will be required.

5. The trustee may be authorized to disclaim the right to the benefits, in which case the benefits may then be paid to a marital deduction trust or directly to John, depending upon the beneficiary designation form.

6. Designating the credit shelter trust as beneficiary is appropriate if Mary has no other assets to fund the credit shelter trust.

7. If there are other assets that will not be treated as income in respect of a decedent (IRD) that can be allocated to the credit shelter trust or directly to children or other beneficiaries, generally more wealth will escape estate taxation in John's estate if the plan benefit is allocated to him or a trust qualifying for the marital deduction, since John or the trust will be paying the income tax on the distributions rather than the credit shelter trust or the children.

QUESTION I-3.

Assume that, instead of being married for 40 years to John, Mary's first husband died when Mary was 55 and she married John when she was 60. Assume also that Anne is Mary's daughter by her prior marriage. How might these facts affect Mary's choice of a designated beneficiary, assuming that the plan benefit constitutes most of Mary's wealth?

ANSWER:

Mary should consider naming a QTIP trust as the beneficiary of her plan benefit. If she wants to qualify the plan benefit for the marital deduction in order to defer the federal estate tax on the benefit as long as possible, but does not want to give John control over the plan benefit remaining at his death, she should name a trust designed to qualify for the marital deduction as the beneficiary. Because her goal is to reduce John's control over the plan benefit, the trust should be a qualified terminable interest property (QTIP) trust. Only a QTIP trust assures Mary of ultimate control over the disposition of any remaining assets in the trust at John's death, including any plan benefit that was treated as principal and retained in the trust and any balance remaining in the plan. An estate trust, which qualifies for the marital deduction, requires that any remaining assets in the trust be payable to John's estate. A life income/general power of appointment trust requires that John have the right either to withdraw the assets from the trust during his lifetime or to designate where the assets in the trust will go at his death.

If the spouse has a right to require the trustee to convert the assets of the QTIP trust to income-producing property or to distribute other trust assets equal to the income that would have been produced by the unproductive property, the value of an IRA or plan benefit payable to the trust should qualify for the marital deduction regardless of whether current income from the IRA or plan benefit is required to be paid to the trust. Normally the beneficiary of an IRA has the right to withdraw the entire account balance at any time and in many qualified retirement plans the beneficiary may have the same right.

Under Revenue Ruling 2000-2, as long as John has the right to require the trustee of the QTIP trust to withdraw the income generated or deemed to be generated by the assets in the IRA or plan and distribute such income to him, the arrangement will satisfy the income requirement under the regulations.

There are additional considerations if the marital trust is the beneficiary.

1. Rollover treatment will be foreclosed unless John has the right to revoke the trust or a lifetime power to withdraw assets from the trust.

2. Had Mary reached age 50 before 1986, ten-year averaging and capital gain treatment would be available if the distribution qualified as a lump sum distribution. Note that five-year averaging is no longer available after 1999.

3. John's consent to waive his rights under REA will be required.

4. If John disclaims his interest in the trust, the benefit may then be paid to a credit shelter trust or directly to other beneficiaries, such as Anne.

5. The four requirements under the minimum distribution rules concerning trusts should be satisfied if the five-year distribution rule is to be avoided.

6. If any of the remainder beneficiaries is not an individual younger than John, minimum distributions may be accelerated.

QUESTION I-4.

Will Mary have to obtain John's consent if she names someone other than John as the beneficiary of her plan benefit?

ANSWER:

Yes, John will have to consent to the payment of the benefit to someone other than him because of the Retirement Equity Act of 1984. The consent must designate a beneficiary and a form of benefit that may not be changed without John's consent, unless he signs a general consent. His consent must acknowledge the effect of the election and must be witnessed by a plan representative or a notary public.

John may sign a general consent, which expressly permits Mary to change the beneficiary designation or form of payment or both without again obtaining John's consent. A general consent is not permitted unless the plan specifically permits such a consent. The general consent would have to acknowledge that John had the right to limit his consent to a specific beneficiary and a specific optional form of benefit and that he had voluntarily elected to relinquish both of these rights (or, if applicable, either of these rights). If Mary, with John's consent, names a revocable trust as the beneficiary, she could later change the beneficiaries or other terms of the trust without his consent.

Mary's waiver of a qualified joint and survivor annuity or qualified preretirement survivor annuity and John's consent to the waiver will be valid only if made during specific election periods. The waiver of a qualified joint and survivor annuity may be made only during the 90-day period ending on the first day of the period for which the first payment is to be made to Mary (referred to as the *annuity starting date*), and only after Mary has received a notice explaining the qualified joint and survivor annuity. Unless Mary makes an irrevocable election, she may, with John's consent, change the form of benefit after the annuity starting date.

Under the Code, a waiver of a qualified preretirement survivor annuity can be made only on or after the first day of the plan year in which the participant reaches age 35. The regulations permit a participant who has not reached age 35 to make a waiver, but the participant must execute a new waiver after reaching age 35. The age 35 provision does not apply to plans, such as certain profit-sharing plans, that are not required to provide the qualified preretirement survivor annuity and qualified joint and survivor annuity. The spouse may consent to a waiver of his or her right to the death benefit, which is the participant's entire nonforfeitable accrued benefit in such a plan, at any time.

The participant must be permitted to revoke his or her election during the applicable election period, although the plan may require that the spouse's consent to a waiver of the qualified preretirement or joint and survivor annuity not be revocable.

A beneficiary designation executed before August 23, 1984, naming someone other than the spouse as the primary beneficiary, whether or not the spouse consented to the designation, is not valid to deprive the spouse of his or her REA rights. In addition, a consent to a waiver signed before a marriage (such as in a premarital agreement) is not a valid consent according to the regulations. Although one state court has held that a premarital agreement may serve as a valid waiver of the spouse's REA rights, in *Estate of Hopkins*,[1] a number of federal courts have upheld the position taken in the regulations.

In 1993, a New York court, in *Kartiganer v. Bloom*,[2] held that a beneficiary designation signed by an unmarried participant was not nullified when the participant subsequently married, so that when the participant died the person named under the beneficiary designation rather than the spouse was entitled to the participant's death benefits. This case is obviously contrary to the regulations, which state that a deemed waiver by an unmarried participant is null and void if the participant subsequently marries. *See also Callahan v. Hutsell*, 193 U.S. App. Lexis 34005(6th Cir. 1993), *remanding* 813 F. Supp. 541(W.D. Ky. 1992), wherein the Sixth Circuit held that a spouse who signed a premarital agreement waiving her right to the participant's benefits may be required to give up her right pursuant to the contract. Also, the court stated that a premarital agreement may qualify as a valid waiver if it satisfied both the statutory requirements and any plan requirements.

In most of these situations, the problem would have been avoided if the plan document had required that, in order to be entitled to the spousal death benefit mandated by the Code and ERISA, the spouse must be married to the participant throughout the one-year period ending on the date of the participant's death. Although such a requirement is permitted under the Code and ERISA, many plans do not contain such a requirement because of the difficulty in administering such a provision. The plan administrator would have to determine when a participant married his or her spouse before making any payments to the spouse after the participant's death.

If a participant who is about to marry is entering into a premarital agreement, the beneficiary designation form for the plan should be signed and notarized (or witnessed by a plan administrator) and attached to the premarital agreement, and the premarital agreement, along with the

---

[1] *Hopkins Estate*, 574 N.E.2d 230 (Ill. App. Ct. 1991), 14 EBC 1145, *cert. denied*, 580 N.E.2d 115 (Ill. 1991).

[2] *In the Matter of Bloom-Kartiganer Estate*, 599 N.Y.S.2d 188 (1993).

attachment, should be furnished to the plan administrator. Based on dicta in the *Callahan* case, this may be sufficient to render the premarital agreement an effective waiver of the future spouse's rights to the participant's plan benefits. It may also be possible to condition the receipt of other economic benefits provided to the fiancé(e) under the premarital agreement on the fiancé(e)'s cooperation in signing any required waivers after the marriage.

A defined contribution plan, other than a money purchase pension plan, is not required to provide the qualified survivor annuities to a participant's spouse if it meets the following requirements:

1. The plan provides that the participant's nonforfeitable accrued benefit (reduced by any security interest held by the plan by reason of a loan outstanding to the participant) is payable in full on the death of the participant to the participant's surviving spouse (or, if there is no surviving spouse or the surviving spouse consents as described earlier, to a designated beneficiary);

2. The participant does not elect to receive the benefits in the form of a life annuity; and

3. With respect to the participant, the plan is not a direct or indirect transferee of a transfer after December 31, 1984, from a plan that is required to provide the qualified joint and survivor annuity and qualified preretirement survivor annuity. When there has been such a transfer, if the transferee plan separately accounts for the transferred assets and income therefrom, the balance of the participant's account is not subject to the survivor annuity rules.

In addition, an employee stock ownership plan (ESOP) is not subject to the qualified survivor annuity rules to the extent a participant has a right to demand a distribution of employer securities. IRAs, simplified employee pension plans (SEPs), and simple retirement accounts (SIMPLEs) are not subject to the spousal consent rules at all.

QUESTION I-5.

Assume that Mary desires to leave $500,000 to the University of Richmond to establish a chair in estate planning and the only other asset in her own name is stock in IBM that has a basis of $100,000 and a current fair market value of $500,000. Could Mary's desire to make this bequest affect her decision concerning the choice of a designated beneficiary?

ANSWER:

Mary should use part of the plan benefit to satisfy her desire to make a gift to the University.

1. When the participant desires to make a substantial gift to charity, using a qualified retirement plan benefit or IRA to satisfy that desire may be advisable since the charity will not be subject to income tax when the benefit or IRA is paid to the charity. Because the IBM stock will get a step-up in basis while the plan benefit will not, if John receives the stock, he may immediately sell the stock without recognizing any taxable income, but would have taxable income to the extent of any plan benefit received in excess of any IRD deduction for estate tax attributable to the benefit.

2. To avoid recognition of the income by the estate, the benefits should not be used to fund a pecuniary charitable bequest, unless the will requires the use of the benefit to satisfy the bequest (Code § 642(c)). For example, Mary's estate would recognize $500,000 of taxable income if her executor uses part of her plan benefit to satisfy a $500,000 cash bequest to the university contained in Mary's will.

   a. Some commentators believe that the satisfaction of a pecuniary bequest with a plan benefit or IRA will not accelerate income recognition because the recipient is only taxable when the benefit or IRA is actually received.

3. The portion of plan benefit payable to the university will be deductible in determining Mary's federal taxable estate as a charitable deduction. A Chief Counsel Advice has taken the position that the satisfaction of a pecuniary bequest to a charitable organization with an interest in an IRA results in current recognition of income and no offsetting charitable deduction.[3]

[3] CCA 200644020.

4. John's consent to waive his spousal rights under the Code and ERISA will be required.

PART II

Assume that four years have elapsed (it is now December 15, 2019), and Mary is now seeking your advice on how to receive her benefits, since she will be required to begin receiving her benefits on or before April 1, 2020 (her required beginning date). Mary wants to defer the receipt of any distributions from the plan for as long as possible, since her current compensation from Good Products allows her and John to live according to the standard which the two of them have enjoyed for a number of years.

QUESTION II-1.

In what form should Mary begin to receive her benefits?

ANSWER:

If Mary and John can afford to do without the cash in her plan, then withdrawal of the plan benefit should be deferred as long as possible under the minimum distribution rules. The amount that would have been paid in income tax on a current distribution will continue to be invested. The income tax on the earnings of the entire amount, including the amount that would have been paid as income tax on a current distribution, will be deferred until the distribution is actually made, causing the amount retained in the plan to increase more rapidly. Deferral may cause the future distributions to be taxed at a higher tax rate if Congress again raises rates. However, the benefit of the tax-free accumulation of income should offset the effect of higher rates after a few years.

QUESTION II-2.

When should Mary begin receiving her benefits? (Should she wait until her required beginning date to receive the first payment?)

ANSWER:

Mary's required beginning date, as mentioned, is April 1, 2020. If she waits until 2020 to receive the first distribution, she will be required to receive two distributions in 2020, one on or before April 1, 2020, to satisfy the required distribution for the year in which she reached age 70½ (2019), and another distribution by December 31, 2020, to satisfy the required distribution for the year 2020. This may push Mary into a higher federal income tax bracket.

In Questions II-3 through II-6, assume that John makes a spousal rollover.

QUESTION II-3.

If Mary dies before John, what will be the effect of naming his daughter Anne, who is now age 40, as his designated beneficiary on the amount of the required payments to John once he reaches his RBD?

ANSWER:

As a result of the new regulations, the amount paid to John during his lifetime will not be affected by naming his daughter Anne as his new designated beneficiary, since payments will be made pursuant to the uniform distribution period table unless John remarries someone who is more than 10 years younger than he is and he names the new spouse as his designated beneficiary.

QUESTION II-4.

If Mary dies before John, and John dies in the year 2021 (before his RBD, which is April 1, 2023), and he has named Anne as his designated beneficiary, over what period must the remaining balance be paid to Anne?

ANSWER:

The payments may be made to Anne over her life expectancy, determined in the year following the year of John's death and reduced by one year for each year thereafter, if the payments commence by December 31, 2022 (the calendar year following John's death).

QUESTION II-5.

If Mary dies before John and John dies on June 1, 2024 (after his RBD), over what period must the remaining balance be paid to Anne?

ANSWER:

The payment may be made over Anne's remaining life expectancy, determined in the year following the year of John's death, reduced by one for each year thereafter, if the payments commence by December 31, 2025 (the calendar year following John's death). However, if John did not receive his required minimum distribution for 2025 before he died, Anne would have to receive that benefit before the end of 2025.

QUESTION II-6.

When must Anne begin receiving the payments after John dies?

ANSWER:

Regardless of whether John dies before or after his RBD, Anne must begin receiving payments before December 31 of the year following John's death. However, if John died after his RBD but before receiving his required distribution for the year in which he died, Anne would be required to receive the required distribution that would have been paid to John if he had not died.

APPENDIX H

List of Acronyms

DEFRA	Deficit Reduction Act of 1984
EGTRRA 2001	Economic Growth and Taxpayer Relief Reconciliation Act of 2001
ERISA	Employee Retirement Income Security Act of 1974
ESOP	Employee Stock Ownership Plan
GST	Generation-Skipping Transfer
IRA	Individual Retirement Account
IRD	Income in Respect of a Decedent
MDIB	Minimum Distribution Incidental Death Benefit
PBGC	Pension Benefit Guaranty Corporation
PPA	Pension Protection Act of 2006
QDOT	Qualified Domestic Trust
QDRO	Qualified Domestic Relations Order
QTIP	Qualified Terminable Interest Property
RA 87	Revenue Act of 1987
RBD	Required Beginning Date
REA	Retirement Equity Act of 1984
RRA 89	Revenue Reconciliation Act of 1989
SEP	Simplified Employee Pensionplan
SRA	Simple Retirement Account
TAMRA	Technical and Miscellaneous Revenue Act of 1988
TEFRA	Tax Equity and Fiscal Responsibility Act of 1982
TRA 86	Tax Reform Act of 1986
TRA 97	Taxpayer Relief Act of 1997
UCA 92	Unemployment Compensation Amendments of 1992

APPENDIX I

Table of Cases

APPENDIX J

Table of Revenue Rulings

APPENDIX K

Table of Private Letter Rulings

APPENDIX L

Table of IRS News Releases, Notices, and Revenue Procedures

News Releases

89-31	57
91-12	54

Notices

83-23	28, 30
87-13	60
89-25	25, 27, 60, 117
97-10	105
97-11	115

Revenue Procedures

97-41	129

Index